PARENTS' COMPLETE GUIDE TO YOUTH SPORTS

Ronald E. Smith, Ph.D.
Frank L. Smoll, Ph.D.
and
Nathan J. Smith, M.D.

University of Washington

A PROJECT OF
The National Association Of
Sport And Physical Education

AN ASSOCIATION OF
The American Alliance For
Health, Physical Education, Recreation,
And Dance.

HDL PUBLISHING COMPANY
A Division of
HDL COMMUNICATIONS
Costa Mesa, CA 92626

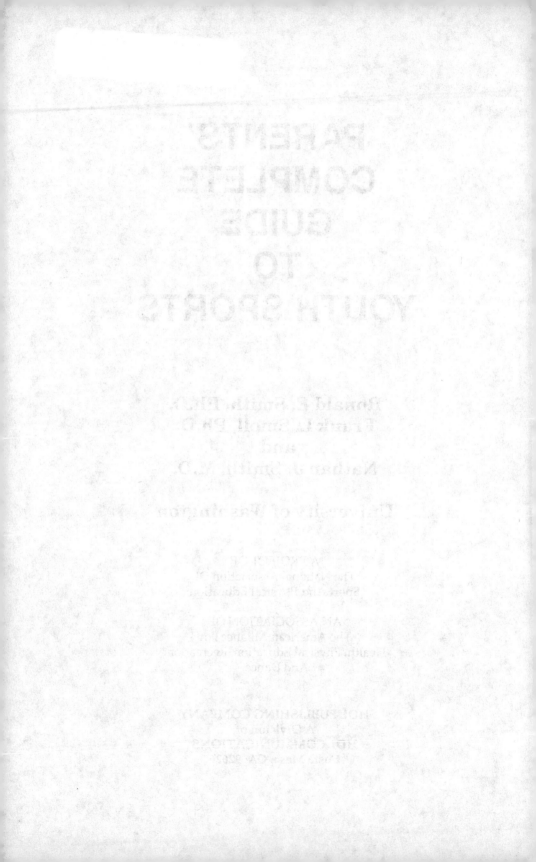

PARENTS' COMPLETE GUIDE TO YOUTH SPORTS

Ronald E. Smith, Ph.D.
Frank L. Smoll, Ph.D.
and
Nathan J. Smith, M.D.

University of Washington

Parents' Complete Guide to Youth Sports
Ronald E. Smith, Ph.D., Frank L. Smoll, Ph.D., Nathan J. Smith, M.D.

Library of Congress Cataloging-in-Publication Data

Smith, Ronald Edward, 1940-
    Parents' complete guide to youth sports.

    "A project of the National Association of Sport and Physical Education, an association of the American Alliance for Health, Physical Education, Recreation, and Dance."
    1. Sports for children.   2. Sports for children—Psychological aspects.   3. Parent and child.
I. Smoll, Frank L.   II. Smith, Nathan J., 1921-
III. National Association of Sport and Physical Education.   IV. Title.
V. Title: Youth sports.
GV709.2.S56 1989   796'.01'922   88-32823
ISBN 0-937359-47-5

Published by
HDL Publishing
A Division of HDL Communications, Inc.
702B Randolph Avenue
Costa Mesa, California 92626
(714) 540-5775

Cover Design by Mike Dirham
Photo of Dr. Smoll by Mary Levin
Photo of Don James by UW Athletic Department
Photos by Jim Kirby and Authors

The National Association of Sport and Physical Education would like to express appreciation to Manufacturer's Life for their support of this publication and quality youth sport programs.

10   9   8   7   6   5   4   3   2   1
Printed in the United States of America

FOREWORD

Sports touch nearly every family, and often they originate in a youth program. Although I am a college football coach, I have had two children participate in youth sport programs, and a third is participating now. I regret not having had an opportunity to read *Parents' Complete Guide to Youth Sports* before they became involved.

Youngsters entering sports for the first time usually are participating for the enjoyment and camaraderie of being with their friends. But when my children started in youth sports, I can remember being extremely upset with the attitudes and conduct of parents toward officials, coaches, and even their own youngsters. There is a tendency among parents to become children's severest critics, when in most cases what a young athlete needs is a pat on the back, not criticism.

Parents' Complete Guide to Youth Sports offers suggestions on what role parents should assume from the time their youngster starts youth sports through recruitment by college coaches. It offers suggestions not only to the parents of gifted athletes but also to parents who have youngsters of average athletic ability. It provides helpful information about parenting young athletes at all levels.

Although only a small percentage of young athletes will be recruited by colleges and universities, for those who are and for their parents, it can be a very trying and emotional period. It is a time when proper input from parents can help a young athlete through a very stressful period and help him or her make a correct decision on which university to attend.

Athletics can be a very enjoyable experience for parents and athletes, or they can become a source of tension and frayed nerves for both. *Parents' Complete Guide to Youth Sports* provides information and guidelines for decision making that can help make youth sports what they should be—an enjoyable and enriching experience for all.

Don James
Parent and head football coach,
University of Washington
1977 College Football Coach of the Year

CONTENTS

viii

CHAPTER 1

CHAPTER 1
YOU AND YOUR CHILD IN SPORTS:
Sanity and Madness in Competition

Dear Mom and Dad:

I'm writing this letter because you've always told me to tell you if anything was bothering me. This has been on my mind for a while, but I haven't been able to get myself to talk about it.

Remember the other night when my team was playing and you were sitting and watching? Well, I hope you won't get mad at me, but you kind of embarrassed me. Remember when I struck out with the bases loaded? I felt really bad about that, but even worse when I heard you yelling at the umpire. Actually, the pitch was a strike, but that pitcher is so fast I just couldn't swing. Then later in the game when the coach took me out in the fourth inning so Danny could play, I really felt bad that you got down on him, because he's trying to do a good job. He really loves baseball and loves coaching us kids.

Dad, I know you want me to be a good ballplayer like you were, and I really do try as hard as I can. But I guess I just can't measure up to what you want me to be. The way you act when I don't do good, it makes me feel like I've let you down. On the way home the other night, neither of you spoke to me. I guess you were pretty sore at me for messing up. You made me feel like I never wanted to play baseball again.

Even though I'm not very good, I love to play and it's lots of fun being with the other kids. But it seems like the only time you're happy is when I do really good—even though you told me that playing sports was supposed to be for fun and to learn the game. I want to have fun, but you keep taking the fun away. I didn't know you were going to get so upset because I couldn't become a star.

This is really hard to say, and that's why I have to write it to you. I used to be really happy that you came to our games. Some of the kids' parents never show up. But maybe it would be better if you stopped coming so I wouldn't have to worry about disappointing you.

Love,
Chris

Chris's letter leaves little doubt that his parents are having a real impact on his youth sport experience. Unfortunately, it is not the kind of effect that one would wish for him. Perhaps Chris's parents are lucky, for their son has the courage to give them feedback on something that is bothering him deeply and influencing his enjoyment of sports. Maybe they can change their behavior, after realizing how they are unintentionally becoming a source of stress rather than a source of support. Like all parents, they want the best for their child, and they may honestly feel that they are supporting him in his sport activities. It also seems clear that there needs to be a change in their attitudes and behavior, if sports are to bring Chris and his parents closer together and to contribute to his enjoyment of the activity.

This book is for you, the parent of the young athlete. We wrote it because we believe that sport participation has great potential for improving the growth and personal development of children and for enriching the family. Because sports are so important to youngsters, what parents do and say in relation to athletics can have an important long-term impact on the child. We hope that this book will provide you with information that will help make the sport experience constructive and enjoyable!

Parents can be a source of support or they can create stress for young athletes.

All parents do as well as they can, within the limits of their awareness. We believe that the information in these pages will increase your awareness of, and help you deal more effectively with, the many problems and opportunities that can arise in youth sports. We welcome the opportunity to increase the knowledge of parents who have a strong background in sports as well as those who have relatively little athletic experience.

The Growth of Youth Sports

How big are youth sports, and how did they get that way? Organized youth sports in the United States actually go back to the early 1900s. The first programs were established in public schools when it was recognized that physical activity was an important part of education. Over time, sponsorship and control of some sports have shifted to a variety of local and national youth agencies. These programs have flourished, and today more children are playing than ever before.

**Youth sports are deeply rooted in our social and
cultural heritage.**

How fast have youth sports grown? Very fast! Little League
Baseball, one of the oldest programs, is a good example. It origi-
nated in 1939 in Williamsport, Pennsylvania, as a three-team league
for eight- to twelve-year-old boys. The program was so popular
that it spread rapidly. By 1949, more than 300 Little Leagues (composed of mostly four teams) were operating in eleven states. In
1987, there were some 16,000 chartered leagues in twenty-five
countries and territorial possessions around the world. Their en-
rollment included more than 2.5 million boys and girls six to eighteen years of age.

Programs in other sports have also shown rapid growth. Esti-
mates of the number of young people (ages six to eighteen) participating in non-school athletics are astonishing. A report presented
at the 1984 Olympic Scientific Congress indicated that about 20 million of the 45 million youth in this age range participate in non-
school sports. In addition, the National High School Federation
estimated that 3.35 million boys and 1.78 million girls, or a total of
5.13 million young people, participated in high school sports. At
the same time, approximately 2.5 million Canadian youth between
the ages of six and eighteen participated in organized team and individual sports.

Growth of the sports movement has demanded the involvement of increasing numbers of adults. Nearly 2.5 million men and
women volunteer their time as coaches, league administrators, and
officials. As programs become more highly organized, parental involvement, of necessity, must also increase.

The youth sport explosion has touched children and adults in
increasing numbers. Several factors have contributed to the rise of
organized youth sports.

- Over the years there has been a clear recognition of
  the importance of wholesome leisure-time activities
  for children.

- The mushrooming of large cities has decreased the
  amount and availability of play spaces.

- Many authorities have looked to sport programs as a
  way of reducing juvenile delinquency.

- Sports have become an increasingly central part of our culture and personal lives. We have become more fitness-minded, and the mass media has brought sporting events into homes of virtually every family.

- The final factor accounting for the growth of youth sports is the most important one. Sports are an enjoyable and rewarding pastime. The most important reason why people participate in sports is that sports can and should provide fun and enjoyment!

Growth in the popularity and scope of youth sports and in the role that they play in the lives of children is undeniable. But this expansion has generated ongoing and, at times, bitter debate. Serious questions have been raised about the desirability of organized sports for children. Unfortunately, answers to the questions are not simple.

Organized Youth Sports: The Debate Lingers On

We have already identified some of the reasons for the rapid growth of youth sports. Obviously this growth could not have occurred if people did not believe that participation in organized sports is beneficial. Those who favor sport programs emphasize that there are many aspects of the experience that contribute to personal development. Some supporters have pointed out that sports are miniature life situations—ones in which children can learn to cope with many of the important realities of life. Within sports, children exercise to cooperate with others, to compete, to deal with success and failure, to learn self-control, and to take risks. Important attitudes are formed about achievement, authority, and persistence in the face of difficulty.

Adult leadership can be one of the truly positive features of organized sport programs. Knowledgeable coaches can help children acquire physical skills and begin to master a sport. Higher levels of physical fitness can be promoted by such guidance. The coach can become a significant adult in the life of the child and can have a huge positive influence on personal and social development. Likewise, the involvement of parents can bring families closer together and heighten the value of the experience for young athletes.

**Sport programs for children have both desirable
and undesirable consequences.**

Youth sports have more than their share of critics. Most notably, coverage by the popular media is dominated by attacks on sport programs. Because mistreatment of children is newsworthy, sport abuses are likely to be sensationalized and widely publicized. Distortions frequently occur. One prominent sport psychologist recently spent ninety minutes with a reporter. For eighty minutes he discussed the positive aspects of sport programs, and for ten minutes he talked about the problems in youth sports. The newspaper article dealt only with the problems. Furthermore, it misquoted the expert as saying that all organized sports should be eliminated for children under the age of sixteen. The media's over-emphasis on the negative has understandably made some parents question the value of youth sports.

Undoubtedly problems can arise in sport programs, and some of these problems have been the focus of severe criticism. *Newsweek* once published a thoughtful editorial by former major league pitcher Robin Roberts, entitled "Strike Out Little League." This Hall of Fame baseball star pointed out that Little League Baseball can place excessive physical and psychological strains on youngsters, and that programs sometimes exist more for the self-serving needs of adults than for the welfare of children. Experts in child development have claimed that adult-supervised and highly organized programs can rob children of the creative benefits of spontaneous play. They suggest that children would benefit far more if adults simply left them to their own games and activities.

Many complaints center around the role of adults in youth sport programs. Critics have charged that some coaches are absorbed in living out their own fantasies of building sport dynasties, and that consequently they show little personal concern for their athletes. Likewise, opponents of youth sports maintain that some parents live through their children's accomplishments and place some tremendous pressure on them to succeed. When coaches and parents become more focused on themselves than on the quality of the children's experience, something is undoubtedly wrong!

The negative involvement of adults in sports has been linked to such problems as the inappropriate use of drugs for training and conditioning purposes, physical injury due to excessive training and competition, and blatant cheating and dishonesty. The

Los Angeles Times reported that one misguided coach injected oranges with amphetamines, then fed them to his ten- to twelve-year-old football players to get them "up" for a game. The *Washington Post* carried a story about a mother who forged a phony birth certificate for her seventeen-year-old son so that he could star in a league for fourteen-year-olds.

Who's right? Are youth sports a symptom of a serious, widespread social disease? Or are they the salvation of our youth? The answer is neither. No reasonable person can deny that important problems do exist in some programs. Some of the criticisms are well founded and can be constructive. On the other hand, surveys have shown that the vast majority of adults and children involved in sports find them to be an enjoyable and valued part of their lives. The bottom line is that sport programs are what we make of them. They can become a source of joy and fulfillment in the life of a child, or a source of stress and disappointment.

A realistic appraisal of youth sports includes recognition of their positive and negative features.

We believe that sports have a strong positive *potential* for achieving important objectives. The question is not whether youth sports should continue to exist—they are here to stay as a firmly established part of our society. If anything, they will continue to grow in spite of the criticisms that are sometimes leveled at them. The real question is how parents can help ensure that sports will be a positive experience for their children.

What can you do to help achieve the many desirable outcomes that are possible? Perhaps the key to unlocking the potential of youth sports lies in being well informed about their physical and psychological dimensions. We hope that the information presented in this book will assist you in your role as a successful youth sport parent.

The Rights of Child Athletes

When children enter a sport program, they automatically assume responsibilities. But they also have rights. Adults need to respect these rights if young athletes are to have a safe and rewarding sport experience. The National Association for Sport and Physical Education's Youth Sports Task Force has developed a "Bill of Rights for Young Athletes." The rights identified by these medical experts, sport scientists, and national youth sport administrators are presented in the accompanying box.

Bill of Rights
for Young Athletes

1. Right to participate in sports.

2. Right to participate at a level commensurate with each child's maturity and ability.

3. Right to have qualified adult leadership.

4. Right to play as a child and not as an adult.

5. Right to share in the leadership and decision-making of sport participation.

6. Right to participate in safe and healthy environments.

7. Right to proper preparation for participation in sports.

8. Right to an equal opportunity to strive for success.

9. Right to be treated with dignity.

10. Right to have fun in sports.

We believe that the "Bill of Rights" provides a sound framework for fulfilling adult responsibilities toward young athletes. These rights will be dealt with in greater detail throughout the book as we explore their implications for enriching the sport experience.

Goals and Models in Youth Sports

What do you want your child to get out of sports? What are the goals that you would like achieved? Parental objectives can range from simply providing a worthwhile leisure-time activity for children to laying the foundation for becoming an Olympic champion or professional athlete. Of course, there are many other goals that may well be more appropriate. Some of them are physical, such as attaining sport skills and increasing physical fitness. Others are psychological, such as developing leadership skills, self-discipline, respect for authority, competitiveness, cooperativeness, sportsmanship, and self-confidence. These are many of the positive attributes that fall under the heading of "character."

"The greatest contribution that sports can make to
young athletes is to build character. The greatest
teacher of character is on the athletic field."
Tom Landry, professional football coach

Youth sports are also an important social activity in which children make new friends and acquaintances and become part of an ever-expanding social network. Furthermore, sports can serve to bring families closer together.

Whatever your objectives may be, it is important that you become aware of them. And you must realize that none of these objectives can be achieved as a result of mere participation in sports. Simply placing a child into a sport situation does not guarantee a positive outcome. The nature and quality of the program, which are very much dependent on the input of adults, are prime factors in determining benefits.

Unlike youth sports, the major goals of professional sports are directly linked to their status in the entertainment industry. Former Dallas Cowboys wide receiver Peter Gent recalled that at the end of rookie camp, a meeting was held to explain the responsibilities of a professional athlete. "The man to give the best advice was the team's public relations director," Gent said. "He told us, 'Boys, this is show business.'"

The goals of professional sports, simply stated, are to entertain and, ultimately, to make money. Financial success is of primary importance and depends heavily on a product orientation, namely, winning. Is this wrong? Certainly not! As a part of the entertainment industry, professional sports have tremendous value in our society.

In the professional sports world, players are commodities to be bought, sold, and traded. Their value is based on how much they contribute to winning and profit-making. They are the instruments of success on the field and at the box office, and they are dealt with as property or as cogs in a machine.

Professional athletes are often glorified by the media to create an image intended to draw paying customers and generate interest in the team. However, many professional athletes feel that little real concern is shown them as human beings or contributing members of society. For example, several professional teams have reportedly turned deaf ears to reports of drug abuse by star athletes as long as the athletes continued to perform well. In his book en-

Professional sports have different goals and values than youth sports.

titled *LT: Living on the Edge*, Lawrence Taylor of the professional football Giants wrote the following about his battle with cocaine addiction: "If they wanted to bust me, fine. But I knew they weren't going to do that, not as long as I was who I was and my game was intact."

"All they seem to care about is what you did for them yesterday and what you can do for them tomorrow."
Willie Mays, Baseball Hall of Famer

The professional coach's job is to win. Those who don't usually join the ranks of the unemployed rather quickly and unceremoniously. No gold watches for years of service, either! A win-at-all-costs philosophy is required for advancement and, indeed, survival. Professional coaches do not receive bonuses for developing character. Their primary function is to help the franchise to compete successfully for the entertainment dollar.

The *developmental model* of sports has a far different focus. As its name suggests, the goal is to develop the individual. The most important product is not wins or dollars but, rather, the quality of the experience for the child. In this sense, sport participation is an educational process whereby children can learn to cope with realities they will face later in life. Although winning is sought after, it is by no means the primary goal. Profit is measured not in terms of dollars and cents but in terms of the skills and personal characteristics that are acquired.

In a developmental model, sports provide an arena for learning, where success is measured in terms of personal growth and development.

We are firmly convinced that most of the problems in youth sports occur when uninformed adults erroneously impose a professional model on what should be a recreational and educational experience for children. When excessive emphasis is placed on winning, it is easy to lose sight of the needs and interests of the young athletes.

We asked earlier what you want your child to get out of sports. Perhaps we also should know about the objectives that young athletes seek to achieve. A sport psychologist, Daniel Gould, summarized the results of two scientific surveys conducted in the United States and Canada. The studies indicated that young athletes most often say they participate in organized sports for the following reasons:

- To have fun
- To improve their skills and learn new skills
- To be with their friends or make new friends
- For thrills and excitement
- To succeed or win
- To become physically fit

Concerned parents should ask their children athletes what *they* want from sports and why *they* wish to participate. Parents should not be guilty of forcing their own aspirations upon their children. Rather, they should make sure that young athletes have a say in determining their own destiny.

It is important to note that the primary goal of the professional—succeeding or winning—is far less important to children. In one of our own studies, we found that teams' won-lost records have nothing to do with how well young athletes liked the coaches they played for or with their desire to play for the same coach again. Interestingly, however, success of the team was related to how much the children thought their parents liked the coach. The children also felt that the won-lost record influenced how much their coach liked them. It appears that even at a very young age, children begin to tune in to the adult emphasis on winning, even though they do not yet share it themselves. *What children do share is a desire to have fun!*

Fun. A term we use a lot. But what is it? Certainly, it's easy to tell when people are having fun. They show it in their expression of happiness, satisfaction, and enthusiasm. We've asked many children why sports are fun for them. Perhaps the most basic reason was given by a little eight-year-old girl who said, "Fun is when I'm doing something that makes me happy just to be doing it, like playing tennis." In other words, much of the fun in sports comes just from performing the activities themselves. One child played on a soccer team that almost never won matches. Yet the youngster could hardly wait for the coming season. Why? Because he had fun. He simply enjoyed playing soccer. Being with others, meeting challenges, feeling the drama of uncertain outcomes, becoming more skilled, all of these add to the fun of doing for doing's sake.

Winning also adds to the fun, but we sell sports short if we insist that winning is the most important ingredient. In fact, several studies reported that when children were asked where they'd rather be—warming the bench on a winning team or playing regularly on a losing team—about 90 percent of them chose the losing team. The message is clear: The enjoyment of playing is more important to children than the satisfaction of winning.

The basic right of the child athlete to have fun in participating should not be neglected. One of the quickest ways to reduce fun is to begin treating children as if they were varsity or professional athletes.

> "It's a disgrace what we're doing in the United
> States and Canada. We're asking kids to compete to
> win. Why not ask them to compete to have fun?
> We're trying to build our own egos on little
> children."
> *Sparky Anderson*, major league baseball manager

Perhaps most importantly, we need to keep in mind that young athletes are not miniature adults. They are children, and they have the right to play as children. In fact, we all do. The Dutch philosopher Johan Huizinga wrote that to play as an adult, everyone must become a child again. Youth sports are first and foremost a play activity, and children deserve to enjoy sports in their own way.

Now, we are not suggesting changing the team names or taking away the uniforms. The youngsters enjoy these trappings. What we are stressing is the need to make sure that our programs remain *child-centered* and do not become adult-centered.

A Winning Philosophy for Youth Sports

Vince Lombardi was a winner. During his years as coach of the Green Bay Packers, he created a professional football dynasty the likes of which had never been seen before. His team was the powerhouse of the NFL during the 1960s—a team driven to near perfection by an intensely competitive, perfectionistic leader. Lombardi's image was immortalized in the famous statement, "Winning isn't everything, it's the only thing."

If you are a sports fan or perhaps even if you are not, you have heard this famous quote. But did you know that Lombardi never actually said that? Years after his death, his son revealed that his father had been misquoted. What Lombardi actually said was, "Winning isn't everything, but striving to win is."

John Wooden was another winner, and so were the UCLA Bruins who played for him. During a twelve-year period from 1963 through 1975, his teams won the national collegiate basketball championship ten times. Certainly, to be that successful Wooden and his Bruins had to be single-mindedly focused on winning games. And yet, at least where Wooden was concerned, this was not the case. In fact, what he did communicate to his teams may have been the key to their success and their ability to play well under pressure. John Wooden once told an audience of coaches:

You cannot find a player who ever played for me at UCLA that can tell you that he ever heard me mention "winning" a basketball game. He might say I inferred a little here and there, but I never mentioned winning. Yet the last thing that I told my players just prior to tip-off, before we would go on the floor, was, "When the game is over, I want your head up, and I know of only one way for your head to be up. That's for you to know that you did your best. No one can do more.... You made that effort."

Yes, Lombardi and Wooden were winners. Their won-lost records speak for themselves. Yet it is interesting to note that both coaches placed an emphasis on the process of striving for excellence. Their visions went beyond a preoccupation with winning games. Instead, they demanded that their players dedicate themselves to 100 percent effort.

The common notion in sports equates success with victory—scoring more points, runs, or goals than the opponent. Yet, in a youth sport model, the measure of a person's or a team's success goes beyond records and standings. Success is a personal thing and is related to one's own standards and abilities. John Wooden captured this relationship when he offered the following definition of success: "Success is peace of mind, which is a direct result of self-satisfaction in knowing you did your best to become the best that you are capable of becoming."

Wooden's perspective on success may be the most important reason why he deserves the title "Wizard of Westwood." He realized that everyone can be a success, because success relates to the effort that one puts into attaining one's personal potential.

In terms of the educational benefits of sports, children can learn from both winning and losing. But for this to occur, winning must be placed in a *healthy* perspective. We have therefore developed a four-part philosophy of winning designed to maximize young athletes' enjoyment of sports and their chances of receiving the positive outcomes of participation.

1. *Winning isn't everything, nor is it the only thing.* Young athletes can't possibly learn from winning and losing if they think the only objective is to beat their opponents. Does this mean that children should not try to win? Definitely not! As a form of competition, sports involve a contest between opposing individuals or teams. It would be naive and unrealistic to believe that winning is not an important goal in sports. But it is not the most important objective.

To play sports without striving to win is to be a dishonest competitor. But despite this fact, it is important that we not define success only as winning. Not every child can play on a championship team or become a star athlete. Yet every child can experience the true success that comes from trying his or her best to win. The opportunity to strive for success is the right of every young athlete.

2. *Failure is not the same thing as losing.* Athletes should not view losing as a sign of failure or as a threat to their personal value. They should be taught that losing a game is not a reflection of their own self-worth. In other words, when an individual or team loses a contest, it does not mean that they are worth less than if they had won. In fact, some valuable lessons can be learned from losing. Children can learn to persist in the face of obstacles and to support each other even when they do not achieve victory.

They can also learn that mistakes are not totally negative but are important stepping stones to achievement. Mistakes provide valuable information that is necessary for improving performance. Thomas Edison was once asked whether he was discouraged by the failure of more than three thousand experiments leading to the development of the light bulb. Edison replied that he did not consider the experiments failures, for they had taught him three thousand ways not to create a light bulb, and each experiment had brought him closer to his goal.

3. *Success is not equivalent to winning.* Thus, neither success nor failure need depend on the outcome of a contest or on a won-lost record. Winning and losing apply to the outcome of a contest, whereas success and failure do not. How, then, can we define success in sports?

4. *Children should be taught that success is found in striving for victory.* The important idea is that *success is related to effort!* The only thing that athletes have complete control over is the amount of effort they give. They have only limited control over the outcome that is achieved. If we can impress on our children that they are never "losers" if they give maximum effort, we are giving them a priceless gift that will assist them in many of life's tasks. A youth soccer coach had the right idea when he told his team, "You kids are always winners when you try your best! But sometimes the other team will score more goals."

"The purpose of organized youth sport programs
should be to teach the child how to play the sport,
about competition, about winning and losing, and
about playing on a team. And the emphasis should
be on the individual going out and enjoying what
he is doing. Every game will have a winner and
loser. The only successful youth sport program is
the one with the coach who will accept the losing
along with the winning, last place in the league
along with the first place, and still be able to
congratulate his team for their efforts."
Roger Staubach, former Dallas Cowboys quarterback

A major cause of athletic stress is fear of failure. When young
athletes know that making mistakes or losing a contest while giving
maximum effort is acceptable, a potent source of pressure is
removed. Moreover, if adults apply this same standard of success
to themselves, they will be less likely to define their own adequacy
in terms of a won-lost record and will more likely focus on the important children's goals of participation, skill development, and
fun. Parents and coaches will also be less likely to experience stress
of their own when their athletes are not winning.

As baseball star Steve Garvey notes, "Competitive stress is
directly related to the emphasis placed on winning by the adult
coach or manager. The object of youth sports is the spirit of competition and the development of sportsmanship. Adult emphasis
on the child to win must be tempered by the belief that competitive effort combined with a sense of fair play will help to alleviate
added stress." When winning is kept in perspective, the child
comes first and winning is second. In this case, the most important
sport product is not a won-lost record; it is the quality of the experience provided for the athletes.

Parent Roles and Responsibilities

Two important sets of adults combine with the child to form
the *athletic triangle*. They are, of course, parents and coaches. The
relationships that exist among the points of the athletic triangle go
a long way toward determining the quality of the experience that
the child has in sports. Being a point in the athletic triangle implies
both rights and responsibilities.

When your child enters a sport program, you automatically
take on some obligations. Some parents do not realize this at first

*Coaches and parents combine with children to form an important
"athletic triangle."*

and are surprised to find out what is expected of them. Others
never realize their responsibilities and therefore miss opportunities
to help their children grow through sports, or actually do things
that interfere with their children's development. In a sense this entire book is about parents' roles and responsibilities. For now, however, we want to summarize some of the more obvious ones.

The right of the child to participate in sports also includes the
right *not* to participate. Although parents might choose to encourage participation, children should not be pressured, intimidated,
or bribed into playing. If youngsters feel forced, their chances of
receiving the benefits of sports are decreased. Even more profound
and long-lasting are the effects which feeling forced can have on
parent-child relationships. An extreme and very sad example of
this is the following statement made to one of us by a New York ex-
ecutive: "If it hadn't been for sports, I wouldn't have grown up
hating my father."

It is possible to be very supportive of a child's athletic interests
without placing demands or pressures on the youngster. For example, hockey great Bobby Orr was fortunate in having very sup-

portive parents. He recalls, "My parents bought my equipment, drove me to the rink, rubbed my feet when they were cold. I can't remember them saying that I was going to be a professional hockey player."

"Parents should be observers and supporters of their athletically inclined children, but never pushers."
Johnny Majors, college football coach

Although coaches have the most direct contact with children within the sport environment, parents also involve themselves to varying degrees. Some parents assume an extremely active role, and sometimes their behavior and the demands they place upon children become a great source of stress for the child. Consider, for example, the following experience described by a youth coach:

One night last season my team lost a close game. I sat the whole team on the bench and congratulated them for trying, for acting like gentlemen. I said I couldn't have been prouder of them if they had won. Most of all, I said, it is as important to be a good loser as a gracious winner. As I talked I could see their spirits lifting. I felt they had learned more than just how to play baseball that night. But as I mingled with the parents in the stands afterward, I was shocked to hear what they were saying to the boys. The invariable theme was, "Well, what happened to you tonight?" One father pulled out a note pad and went over his son's mistakes play by play. Another father dressed down his son for striking out twice. In five minutes the parents had undermined every principle I had set forth.

It is natural for parents to identify with their children to some extent, to take pleasure in their triumphs, and to suffer in their defeats and disappointments. The love bond that exists between parent and child virtually guarantees this process. Like all good things, however, this process of identification can become excessive so that the child becomes an extension of the parent. When this happens, parents may begin to define their own success and self-worth in terms of how successful their child is, as in the following cases.

Tommy's father never was a good athlete. Now in his adult years, he is a "frustrated jock" who tries to experience through Tommy the success he never knew as an athlete. Tommy is pushed to excel, to put in long hours of practice, and to give up other activities. When he performs poorly, his father becomes withdrawn and gloomy. Dad takes home movies of Tommy during practices and games, and visitors to the home are promptly shown some of Tommy's triumphs. Tommy himself is a reasonably good athlete at age twelve, but he is unlikely ever to become a superstar. In fact, a school-teacher has become very concerned because Tommy "doesn't seem himself" and is lagging in his schoolwork. The family's physician is concerned even more, because Tommy has been complaining of abdominal pains and the doctor is fearful he may be developing an ulcer.

Sheila's mother was a champion collegiate swimmer who won a bronze medal in the Olympic Games. It is clear that the mother expects Sheila to follow in her footsteps. Sheila was a "waterbaby" at six months of age and was "in training" by age four. She shows every sign of becoming a high-level competitor in her own right. She is now ten years of age and has won countless medals in age-group swim competitions. Her mother clearly is delighted with and totally engrossed in her athletic development. But her father is becoming worried. Lately, Sheila doesn't seem to enjoy swimming as much. Last week she announced that she wanted to stop training and go to summer camp with some friends for several weeks. Her mother flatly refused to consider this, and Sheila burst into tears, saying that she didn't want to swim anymore. Sheila's father is concerned that her mother is placing so much pressure on the child to excel that she is experiencing burnout.

Tommy and Sheila are showing clear signs of the stress caused when parents try to live through their children. Tommy is being pushed to become the great athlete that his father always wanted to be, and Sheila is having to measure up to the standards set by her mother as a champion athlete. These children *must* succeed or their parents' self-image is threatened and the children themselves are threatened with disapproval or loss of love. Much more is at stake than a mere game or swim meet, and the child of such a parent carries a heavy burden.

Parents can be a potent source of athletic stress.

At some level both Tommy and Sheila must be aware that their parents' happiness depends on how well they perform. Children are accustomed to being dependent on their parents and are often unequipped to handle a reversal of the dependency relationship. This is especially the case when the parent is demanding winning results rather than the best effort of which the child is capable.

We should point out that sports are not the only activities in which this may occur. The performance arena may be in academics, music, dance, or social popularity—any activity that has social or personal importance for the parent. But because of the importance of sports in our society, and particularly in the world of many parents, there is special potential for the dependency-reversal process to occur in the realm of sports.

One of the most important responsibilities of childrearing is the role that parents play in shaping their children's perceptions and understanding of their world. Sports can be a proving ground for later life experiences. Therefore, you have the opportunity to help your young athlete accurately interpret and understand sport experiences and place them in a proper and healthy perspective. For example, you can play a key role in helping your child understand the significance of winning and losing, of success and failure. You can help your child define his or her success in terms of effort expended instead of the score at the end of the contest. Moreover, winning or losing a contest may be the result of external factors beyond the child's control, such as officials, weather, other players, or luck. Or it may be the result of internal causes, such as the child's ability and effort. By helping children to accurately interpret the causes of sport outcomes, parents help youngsters view the world more realistically.

There are other important challenges that must be met by youth sport parents. To contribute to the success of a program, you must be willing and able to commit yourself in many different ways. The following questions serve as important reminders of the scope of parents' responsibilities. You should be able to honestly answer "yes" to all the questions.

Can you give your child some time? You will need to decide how much time you can devote to your child's activity. It may involve driving children to and from practice, going to your child's games, meets, or matches, and assisting the coach. Many parents do not realize how much time can be consumed by such activities. Some parents who expect sport programs to occupy their child's time and give them more time for themselves are shocked to find that they are now spending more time with their children than before. Conflicts arise when parents are very busy, yet are also interested and want to encourage their children. Thus, one challenge is to deal honestly with the time-commitment issue and *never promise more time than you can actually deliver.*

Can you accept your son's/daughter's triumphs? Every child athlete experiences "the thrill of victory and the agony of defeat" as part of the competition process. Accepting a child's triumphs sounds easy, but it is not always so. Fathers, in particular, may be competitive with their sons. This process is the opposite of the over-identification discussed earlier. For example, when Jack played well in a basketball game, his father pointed out minor mistakes, described how other players did even better, and then reminded his son of even more impressive sport achievements of his own. This reestablished his role as a dominant parent and thoroughly deflated Jack.

Can you accept your son/daughter's disappointments? Disappointments are also part of sports and they may be keenly experienced by your child at times. Would you be embarrassed if your child

Parents must be ready to respond to their athlete's dissappointments as well as triumphs.

broke into tears after a tough loss or after making a mistake? Could you put your arm around and comfort your child at such a moment? Can you tolerate becoming a target for young child's displaced anger and frustration when there is no other outlet for disappointment and hurt? When an apparent disappointment occurs, parents should be able to help their children see the positive side of the situation. By doing this, you can change your child's disappointment into self-acceptance. Again, emphasizing effort rather then outcome can be an important means to this goal.

Can you show your child self-control? Conduct at practices and during contests (games, meets, matches) can have an important impact on your child. Parents who yell at or criticize athletes, coaches, or officials set an incredibly poor example for their youngsters. You are a significant role model for your child in all aspects of life, including sports. It is not surprising to find that parents who exhibit poor self-control in their own lives often have children who are prone to emotional outbursts and poor self-discipline. If we are to expect sportsmanship and self-control from our children, we need to exhibit the same qualities in our own behavior.

A careful man I want to be,
A little fellow follows me.
I do not dare to go astray,
For fear he'll go the selfsame way.
Sam Rutigliano, college football coach

Can you let your child make his or her own decisions? One of the opportunities that sport provides is the chance for children to acquire and practice adult behaviors. An essential part of growing up is accepting responsibility for one's own behavior and decisions. This can become a real challenge for parents because once you invite your child to make decisions, you must support and live with those decisions. As a child matures, you should provide encouragement, suggestions, and guidance about sports. But ultimately, within reasonable limits, parents should let their children become more independent and self-reliant. For example, making commitments to a team or program is an important decision, as is a decision to quit a team. At times such as these, parents must accept that they cannot control their children's lives. Decisions about sports can offer parents an introduction to the major process of letting go and allowing their children to become adults in their own right.

Can you give up your child? A final challenge relates to the third point in the athletic triangle, your child's coach or manager: Can you give up your child to another significant adult? Many issues can arise in your relationship with the coach, including the way in which he or she is coaching the team or relating to your child. You are putting your youngster in the charge of another adult and trusting him or her to guide the sport experience. Beyond that, you must deal with the fact that the coach may gain admiration and affection that was once yours alone. It is natural for a coach to become a very important figure in a child's life. This occurs at a time when a tendency toward independence is causing the child to move away somewhat from parents. One father described his difficulty in adjusting to his child's coach:

I was used to being number one in Mark's life. I was the man he looked up to, the man with all the answers, the man to be like someday. Things began to change a bit when he joined the basketball league. He was placed on a team run by the most popular coach in the league, a man who had played college ball and who has a real charisma with kids. All of a sudden, all we heard at the dinner table was, "Coach said this and Coach did that." It became more and more clear that my son had a new hero, and one whom I couldn't compete with. I've thought about it a lot and I can understand that what's happening is perfectly normal, but it's not easy to take a back seat in my child's life, even temporarily.

When parents cannot accept the entry into the child's world of a new and important adult, youngsters may suddenly find themselves in the middle of a conflict between parent and coach in which the child is subtly pressured to make a choice between the two. Like allowing your child more freedom to make decisions, sharing him or her temporarily with another valued adult (and one toward whom greater esteem seems to be shown at times) can be an important part of the process of letting go.

Sports offer your child many opportunities for personal growth and development. They also offers parent and child opportunities to interact in ways that enrich their relationship. It is our hope that this book will contribute to a better understanding of you and your child in sports.

A Child's Plea

Well, here it is another hockey season,
So I am writing you for just one reason,
Please don't scream or curse and yell,
Remember I'm not in the N.H.L.
I am only 11 years old
And can't be bought or traded or sold,
I just want to have fun and play the game
And am not looking for hockey fame
Please, don't make me feel I've committed a sin
Just because my team didn't win
I don't want to be that great, you see
I'd rather play and just be me
"And so, in closing, I'd like to give you one tip—
Remember, the name of the game is
SPORTSMANSHIP.

Donny Chabot, age eleven
Sault Sainte Marie, Ontario

CHAPTER 2

CHAPTER 2
THE PSYCHOLOGY OF
THE YOUNG ATHLETE:
Mind and Motives

The development of a human being is a truly remarkable process. In only nine months two microscopic cells change into a fully formed human infant. Six years later the newborn has become a walking, talking first-grader ready to master such complex skills as reading, arithmetic, relating to others, and sports. From here, a process of rapid mental, physical, and social development advances the child into the storms and challenges of adolescence and then into such adult roles as worker, husband or wife, and parent.

As parents, we have a window to the wonders of growth and development in our children. We are excited by rapid events of evolving maturity. And, at the same time, we are saddened by the realization that we and our children can never recapture the delights of earlier ages, now preserved only in our photo albums, home movies, and hearts.

Because so much of a child's time is spent in play, the functions of play have attracted the attention of educators, medical doctors, and scientists. To understand the role of sports in the life of the child, we must first consider the meaning and functions of play itself.

Play and the Developing Child

Animals as well as humans engage in play activities. In animals play is a way of learning and rehearsing behaviors that are necessary for future survival. For example, baby lions stalk and pounce on objects in their play. In children, too, play has important functions during development.

From its earliest beginnings in infancy, play is a way in which children learn about the world and their place in it. Much of the first two years of life is spent learning about objects and events. By handling and manipulating objects in the environment, infants gain information about how to respond to the world and how it responds to them.

Between the ages of two and seven, children spend most of their waking hours involved in play. In their play, they take on a variety of imaginary roles. With time, they become responsive to playmates and begin to understand the effects of their actions on them. Play now becomes an important avenue for social development. Children can try out various kinds of social interactions by creating rules for games or by developing ways to cooperate, share, or compete. They can experiment with different roles and actions without actually experiencing the dangers that the real action might hold. Through make-believe play, children can test skills— such as driving a car or cooking a meal—that they might not be allowed to try in reality at that time. They can also learn new skills, such as building with blocks or mastering an electronic video game, by watching more skillful playmates.

Play serves as a training ground for skills, knowledge, and social development.

In later childhood, play changes from the dramatic fantasy of the young child to games regulated by rules that everyone accepts. Beyond age six, children spend a great deal of time making up exact rules, and they place strong pressure on one another to follow them. Through this process children learn that social systems are cemented together by rules and that the good of the group demands the individual's willingness to abide by the rules. This is the beginning of consideration for the rights of others. Children learn to compete, too, but within a safe world where the consequences of losing are minimized. Younger children often attach little significance to who wins or loses. In contrast to many adults, they often get their enjoyment from experiencing, not just from winning.

Self-Concept Development

During the early elementary school years, the world of the child broadens dramatically to include not only the family and playmates but a widening circle of schoolmates and adults. In this expanded environment children discover and judge their own abilities and begin to form a stable self-concept and feelings of self-worth. Academic and social experiences provide important information, as do the reactions of peers and adults in the child's life. It is during this critical period of development—the years between six and twelve—that most children enter organized sport programs. This is why sport experiences can play such an important role in children's personal and social development.

Self-concept consists of what we *believe* about ourselves. It includes our perceptions of personal traits and abilities, particularly those that are important in shaping our identities as distinct people. *Self-esteem* refers to the way we *feel* about our own characteristics— as good or bad, valuable or worthless, and so on. Self-concept and self-esteem strongly influence how we function in the world. They underlie our view of who we are, what we are capable of, and how we can expect others to react to us

None of us was born with a self-concept. It is a product of our experiences in living. Two types of information are particularly important with regard to self-concept and self-esteem development:

- How other people respond to us.

- How we compare with others in important skills and characteristics

From the reactions of significant people in their lives, children draw conclusions concerning how other people feel about or evaluate them. Children often have little more than the reactions of others to go on. It is no wonder that such information has such a strong influence on their sense of who they are and how worthwhile they are. Thus, a child who consistently receives attention, approval, and loving concern from parents is likely to conclude that he or she is a valued person and thereby develops a positive self-concept and high self-esteem. Such messages to the child may be very direct, as when a parent says, "You're a great kid and I love you very much," or they may be transmitted in more subtle ways, such as approving smiles and expressions of attention and interest in the child. On the other hand, children who receive a lot of disapproval, rejection, and hostility from those who matter are likely to infer that others see them as unlovable, unworthy, and inferior. It is not surprising that such children tend to develop negative self-concepts and low self-esteem.

A second important type of information enters into the developing conception of self. At a relatively early age, children begin to compare themselves with other children. This is quite natural, for in any new or novel situation we have little basis for judging ourselves or our performance except in comparison with others. Comparison and competition begin around the age of five or six and increase throughout the elementary school years, with the peak occurring around grades four, five, and six. Through self-comparison and competition with other children, youngsters learn where they stand relative to others like them. It is easy to see how such information would feed into the developing self-concept of the child.

Psychologists who study personality place much emphasis on self-concept because we tend to filter new information and to behave in accordance with our self-concept. We tend to accept evidence that supports our notion of ourselves, be it positive or negative, and reject or explain away evidence that is inconsistent with our self-concept. Thus, a failure may have little impact on a child with a positive view of himself or herself, while the same failure may serve to demonstrate once again to the low-self-esteem youngster how inadequate he or she really is.

Children with poor self-concepts and low self-esteem have little confidence in their abilities. They are insecure in their relationships with others, are highly sensitive to criticism, and are easily hurt. Some try to cover up their feelings of inadequacy with an aggressive or attention-demanding front that alienates others, whereas others withdraw into a protective shell. Either response tends to result in low popularity, and this only serves to confirm a poor self-image. The low-self-esteem youngster is thus primed for entry into a failure cycle.

Sports and Self-Concept Development

We can now see why sport experiences can have an important effect on a child's self-concept development. Children typically enter the world of sports at a time in their development when they are seeking information about their abilities. The kinds of motor abilities required in sports are particularly valued by them at this stage. When children enter sports, the stage is thus set for an ability test whose outcome is potentially very important.

There are good reasons to try to succeed and to be a good athlete. Success brings feelings of mastery, competence and self-pride, admiration and status from peers, and approval from important adults, such as parents and coaches. Inferior athletes often experience feelings of shame and inferiority, lowered respect and status among their peers, and the reactions of disappointed parents.

At the very first practice or tryout, children begin to see how they compare with their peers in this prized activity. In a very short time children can tell how proficient they are relative to their teammates and opponents.

In addition to comparing themselves with others, children also have many opportunities to observe how others are judging them. The reactions of coaches, parents, teammates, opponents, and spectators to their play are visible on many occasions. Some of these evaluations are very direct, as when others offer praise or criticism. Other reactions, although unintentionally shown, are easily picked up by a child. For example, when Bobby comes to the plate with the bases loaded, his teammates, the coach, and spectators cheer and shout, "Hit a home run!" When Chad comes up under the same circumstances, there is silence or maybe even a few groans. Or "encouragement" may take such forms as "C'mon, Chad, try to hit the ball!" or "Don't strike out!"

The sport setting provides many opportunities for self-comparisons and reactions from others.

As youth sport programs become more highly organized, formal procedures, such as grading players during tryouts, "drafting" players, and even buying them with play money, provide direct indications of ability. One child we know was devastated when his coach paid only $25,000 in play money for him while his neighborhood buddy went for $40,000! Even more painful is being cut, a most humiliating message that one doesn't measure up. Research done in Canada by sport scientist Terry Orlick showed that nearly three out of every four nonparticipants who didn't go out for hockey teams said that they were afraid of being cut—an indication of how much children dread the message that they're not good enough.

Even children who make the team continue to receive many messages about their performance. This feedback comes from people whose opinions carry a great deal of weight because they are so important to the child. Many parents are very concerned about their children's athletic development and often have a good deal to say about performance. It is the job of another significant adult, the coach, to evaluate performance. Youngsters receive much feedback from this "expert" about their strengths, weaknesses, areas needing improvement, and progress. The coach also makes very obvious ability judgments in selecting players for particular positions, in choosing who starts and who substitutes, and in deciding the game conditions in which substitutions occur. Being allowed to play only when one's team is way ahead or hopelessly behind communicates a pretty clear message.

Sports provide many opportunities for comparisons with and reactions from important others.

Athletics thus provide many opportunities for children to form judgments about their abilities. They get information by comparing themselves with others as well as by observing the reactions of others to them. All this occurs during the age period when children are beginning to form a stable conception of who they are and how they feel about themselves. If you add to this the fact that motor abilities are of central importance and highly valued at this age and that the people evaluating the child—coaches, peers, and parents— are of great importance in the child's life, is it any wonder why the experiences children have in sports can have a rather profound effect on them? This is particularly the case with children who have not established feelings of self-worth in other areas of their lives or with those whose parents value athletic abilities above all others. Finally, it is important to realize that children at this age are not yet capable of distinguishing between judgments of their abilities and judgments of their personal worth. Thus, ability judgments are not necessarily seen as evaluations of only a single physical trait but may well be taken as an indication of total worth.

What Parents Can Do

It is important that adults be sensitive to the impact that sport experiences can have on the child's developing conception of self.

The processes we have described—self-comparison and feedback from others—are going to occur in any situation in which children interact, but their effects can be softened and viewed more realistically if understanding adults help children place sport experiences in proper perspective. There are several things adults can do.

First and foremost is to emphasize fun, participation, and skill improvement rather than winning and losing. Most children want to play a sport because they enjoy the activity for its own sake. Adults can turn that enjoyable activity into a pressurized, competitive nightmare. Fun is no longer just playing; it's now defined as winning. Introducing material rewards, such as trophies, into the picture can cause children to lose sight of the fun of merely playing.

Second, adults should emphasize striving to improve skills rather than comparing oneself with others. Physical development and skill development occur at different rates in youngsters, and it is important to make this clear to children. It is particularly important that children whose skill development is lagging not view this as a permanent condition. Helping a youngster derive pleasure from his or her improvement over time and praising the self-improvement efforts of the child can create many rewarding experiences in sports, even for the athlete who never will be a star.

Parents should emphasize fun, participation, and self-improvement.

Just as it is important that the unskilled child athlete not develop low self-worth because of his or her own sport abilities, it is important that the highly skilled athlete not acquire an inflated self-image. Again, parents should help children to understand that despite the importance of sports to them, it is only one area of their lives. This will foster a more balanced perspective and a wider range of interests.

Finally, it is important that parents examine the conditions of worth that they hold for their children. If your young athlete must excel to get love and approval from you, if you are sending out subtle (or not so subtle) signals of disapproval when your child fails or embarrasses you, then you need to take a hard look at your own priorities. If, on the other hand, you are able to communicate love and acceptance to your child whether he or she is a star or a bench warmer, then a basis for positive self-concept development exists regardless of your child's eventual success in sports.

Competitive experiences are an important part of life. In themselves, sports are neither good nor bad. The value of competition for the child depends on how the competition is conducted, how the situation is interpreted, and how the outcome of competition is understood. Properly managed, youth sports can be an important training ground for competing successfully in other areas of life and for the development of a positive self-concept.

Sport Motivation and Competitiveness

The concept of motivation is the central one in our attempt to understand the whys of behavior. It helps us to understand differences among people in the goals they pursue and in the vigor with which they pursue them. In sports as in other areas of life, the importance of motivation is well recognized. Motivation is crucial to understanding both sport involvement and performance. As a parent, understanding your child's needs and motives can help you provide a more positive athletic experience for him or her.

There are many reasons why children are drawn to sports. Some of the reasons have to do with the activities themselves. Children, like adults, find it enjoyable to hit a baseball, dribble and shoot a basketball, run and catch a football, kick a soccer ball, or stroke a tennis ball. Using one's body just for the sake of doing so is in itself a joyful activity and provides what psychologists term *intrinsic* motives for participating in sports.

Sport involvement can also be a means of satisfying other important needs. We have already talked about the need to compare ourselves with others in the process of defining our abilities and establishing our self-concept. There are two other psychological needs that sports fulfill: the need for competence and achivement, and the need for recognition and approval.

Achievement-Related Motives

Sports provide many opportunities to demonstrate competence and mastery. It is an area in which competence is highly valued by adults and children alike. We should therefore expect that motives having to do with success and failure would be among the most important determinants of sport participation and performance.

The most universal principle of motivation is that people, like animals, strive for positive or pleasurable things and avoid experiences that are painful or threatening. It thus makes sense to distinguish between *approach* motives and *avoidance* motives. Where achievement is concerned, there are two separate but related motives: the need to achieve, and fear of failure. Research has shown quite clearly that these are separate sources of motivation and that people differ widely in the strength of these two motivational states. Some people are low in both motives, others are high in one and low in the other, and still others are high in both.

The need to achieve is an approach motive. It is a positive desire to attain success and to compete successfully with standards of excellence. Differences in achievement motivation begin to emerge in children in the early school years. Children who are high in achievement motivation seek out challenging situations and are concerned with how well they perform, in terms of both their own standards and the performance of others. They also tend to show a lot of persistence in their attempts to achieve. Failure tends to spur them on to greater effort rather than discourage them. They tend to prefer situations that put their abilities to the test. Many studies have shown that when their achievement motivation is aroused, these children perform at a higher level than those low in achievement motivation.

**Some try to achieve for the thrill of success; others
to avoid the agony of failure.**

The other side of the achievement coin is, of course, failure. Just as some children show a positive desire for success, others exhibit a negative fear of failure. People who have great fear of failure work hard not so much because they yearn for "the thrill of victory" as because they dread "the agony of defeat." For them, achievement situations are not challenges, but threats. The child highly motivated to achieve gets "pumped" and "psyched up" when faced with a challenge, but the child highly motivated by fear of failure is more likely to get "psyched out." Tension, fear, and anxiety result. And although the motivation to achieve tends to improve performance, the fear of failure tends to disrupt it.

How Achievement Motivation and Fear of Failure Develop

Because the motivation to achieve and the fear of failure so strongly affect enjoyment of and performance in achievement situations, researchers have been very interested in understanding how these motives develop. They have found that children who have high levels of achievement motivation but little fear of failure tend to have a history of encouragement and reward for success and independence. Parents of such children tend to emphasize the positive aspects of achievement and to praise their children for their efforts to achieve. Importantly, when their children try hard but nevertheless fail, these parents do not punish or criticize them. Instead, they encourage them to continue their attempts and praise them for their persistence. Because of the emphasis that the parents place on striving to meet standards of excellence, this value is adopted by the children and serves to guide their behavior.

The background of the fear-of-failure child is quite different. These children tend to want to avoid new experiences or activities because of the punishment or rejection associated with previous failures. Their parents tend to focus only on the success or failure experienced by the child, not on the effort the child puts out. They express displeasure with the child when failure occurs but take success for granted and expect it. In some cases, unrealistically high goals are set for the child, and the parents express displeasure when the child does not succeed. It is quite easy to see how such a background would result in a child who has learned to dread failure. Ironically, once the fear develops, its disruptive effects are likely to further decrease the chances of success. What often occurs is a vicious cycle in which failure results in increased anxiety, which in turn helps to ensure future failure.

What Parents Can Do

Sports can be a training ground for the development of positive motivation toward achievement. Parents and coaches can have an important influence on developing attitudes concerning success and failure. Research on the development of the need for achievement and fear of failure offers some pretty clear guidelines for how you can help your child develop a healthy achievement orientation. The key principles seem to be encouraging the child to give maximum effort and rewarding him or her for that effort. Make sure the achievement standards you set are reasonable and within your child's capabilities. When success occurs, enjoy the success with your child and express appreciation for the effort that went into it. *Never* be punitive or rejecting if the child tries but does not succeed. Show your child that you understand how disappointed he or she is, and encourage the child to continue trying. Communicate love and acceptance regardless of success or failure. If you want to avoid developing fear of failure, don't give your child a reason to dread failure.

Understanding Competitiveness

One of the most highly prized athletic traits is competitiveness. Applying what we now know about achievement-related motives helps us to understand what goes into being a good competitor. From youth leagues to professional leagues, outstanding competitors are almost always people who are high in achievement motivation and low in fear of failure. Challenging athletic situations arouse their strong desire to achieve, and unhindered by performance-disrupting fears of failure, they tend to peak under pressure. They enjoy and seek out the challenge of athletic competition.

Quite the opposite occurs in the child who is primarily motivated by fear of failure. Competitive situations provide little to gain but much to lose for such children. If they can avoid competition, they will do so. If other factors force them to compete, they derive little enjoyment from it and their performance tends to deteriorate under pressure. Some children who apparently enjoy sports but who have a great fear of failure tend to like practices and "goofing off" more than they do games.

Besides children with such high-low levels of achievement motivation and fear of failure, there are also children who have high levels of both and those who have low levels of both. The child who has high levels of both motives is in a state of conflict between approach and avoidance motives. This child wants to achieve but

---

Relationships Between Achievement Motivation, Fear of Failure, and Competitiveness

Achievement Motivation

		Low	*High*
Fear of Failure	*Low*	Achievement concerns are largely irrelevant. Appears "laid back" and is probably in sport for reasons unrelated to achievement.	Is a good competitor; peaks under pressure because fear of failure does not disrupt performance. Enjoys and seeks out the challenges of competition and is persistently motivated to win.
	High	Competition is threatening. Experiences anxiety under pressure, which lowers performance. Does not enjoy competition and may avoid such situations by dropping out.	Has conflict in competitive situations. Wants to win but also fears failure, so performance may suffer. Does not enjoy the threatening part of competition.

also fears failure. If the child enjoys the sport itself, he or she tends to remain in it but experiences stress and anxiety under pressure. The key to helping such a child to become a good competitor is to reduce fear of failure so that the positive effects of the motivation to achieve are not interfered with.

For the child who has low levels of both achievement motivation and fear of failure, achievement concerns have little importance. When such children do elect to participate in sports, it is often because they simply enjoy the activity or because of the social benefits of participation. As a result, they exhibit a rather nonchalant attitude about the sport. This can prove perplexing and irritating to parents and coaches who are more concerned about winning and achievement.

Needs for Approval and Recognition

As social beings, humans have a need to be recognized, valued, and cared about by others. From a very early age, children seem to crave attention and to do whatever is necessary to gain it. Many children with behavior problems develop those problems because obnoxious behavior is the only way the children have of guaranteeing the attention of parents and others. Such children prefer the attention that goes along with being punished to simply being ignored.

As children develop they learn to satisfy their needs for recognition and approval in a variety of ways. For one thing, they find out what is praiseworthy to people who matter to them, such as parents, teachers, and peers. It doesn't take most children very long to realize that sports provide many opportunities for recognition and approval. They see how sport heroes are idolized in our culture, and they often develop their own sport heroes at a relatively early age. Further, many parents communicate very positive attitudes about sports and exhibit a great deal of interest in such activities. Finally, as we noted earlier, physical skills are among the most highly prized attributes of school-aged children.

Approval and recognition provide powerful motivation for athletes at all levels. Almost all of the positive attributes that can be developed through sport participation—achievement motivation, sportsmanship, teamwork, unselfishness—are ultimately strengthened through the approval of significant people, such as coaches, parents, and teammates. Thus, it is almost impossible to overestimate the importance of approval and recognition to the developing athlete.

As was the case with achievement, there are both approach and avoidance motives connected with approval. On the approach side, there is the positive desire to obtain approval and recognition from other people. This is similar to the positive achievement motive that we discussed earlier. The child wants approval and may be frustrated if approval is not received, but the child is not necessarily afraid of disapproval.

On the other hand, the social behavior of many people is motivated by a strong desire to avoid disapproval at all costs, a motivational state similar to fear of failure. Such people are very concerned about the evaluation of others, and they are fearful of being evaluated unfavorably. Often they automatically assume that all assessments will be negative. As a result, they may experience considerable tension and distress in social situations, and they may be highly motivated to avoid them. Where fear of disapproval is not excessive, these people enter social situations but strive to please others at all costs. They are highly conforming and hesitate to take a position that others might disapprove of. They define their own self-worth in terms of the feedback they get from other people.

**For child athletes the most important external
sources of approval are coaches, parents, and peers.**

Of equally great importance, however, is the child's own self-approval or self-disapproval. Once children begin to set standards for their own behavior, they approve or disapprove of themselves depending on whether or not they meet these standards. Thus, a young boy may feel badly about himself if he does something that he knows is wrong even if his friends approve. The development of internal standards of behavior and of conditions for self-approval and self-disapproval is a sign of developing maturity in a child.

Motivational patterns differ from child to child, of course, but in a recent research project we tried to determine the relative strength of approval motives in child athletes. We devised a psychological test to measure the approval-related reasons that children strive to do well in sports, and we administered the test to a large number of boys and girls of various ages.

The table on the next page shows the results of this study.

It is noteworthy that for children in both age groups, their own self-approval and self-disapproval were more important to them than the reactions of peers, coaches, or parents. Where parents were

Reasons for Trying to Perform Well in Sports		
Reason for Trying to Play Well	**Order of Importance**	
	9-11	*12-14*
	Years Old	
1. Feeling good about how you played.	1	1
2. Making sure you won't blame yourself for losing.	2	2
3. Being praised by your parents for playing well.	6	4
4. Making sure your parents won't be displeased with your play.	3	8
5. Making your coach proud of you.	4	3
6. Making sure your coach won't be displeased with you.	5	6
7. Making the other kids like you more.	8	7
8. Making sure the other kids don't get upset with you.	7	5

concerned, the younger children were more strongly oriented toward avoiding parental disapproval than toward gaining their approval, whereas the older youngsters were relatively more concerned with getting approval than with avoiding disapproval. It is important to note, however, that this pattern did not hold for all children, but only for the sample as a whole. For some children, the reactions of others were of utmost importance. Sometimes the primary motive was to gain approval, while other children were clearly motivated to avoid the disapproval of others.

The motives that bring children into sports and that affect their development and performance once they get there are of great importance in understanding the child athlete. In subsequent chapters we will return frequently to these motivational factors.

Extrinsic Rewards: Can We Destroy Love of the Game?

The story is told of an elderly woman who lived in an apartment building next to a vacant lot. One afternoon as she was settling down for her daily nap, a frisky group of boys and girls appeared in the vacant lot and began a noisy pickup softball game. The racket was deafening and the children obviously enjoyed the game far more than the old woman did. Her only comfort was the hope that they would not come back. But, alas, the children joyfully returned the next two days as well.

On the third day, as the children were leaving, the woman walked down to the vacant lot and called them together. She told them that she liked to watch and listen to them play and asked them to come back and play noisily in the vacant lot the next day. If they did, she said, she would give each of them a quarter. The children raced back the following day and had a wild game, looking occasionally up at the old woman smiling approvingly from her window. She paid each of them a quarter and asked them to return the next day. Again the next day she paid them after their game. This time, however, she gave each child only twenty cents, explaining that she was running out of money. On the following day, they got only fifteen cents each. Furthermore, she told them, she would have to reduce their payment to five cents the next day. The children became angry and told the woman they would not be back. It was not worth the effort, they said, to play a game for only five cents a day.

The old woman might very well have been a retired psychologist, for she had cleverly used external rewards, in this case money, to decrease the desire of children to play ball. We can assume that the children originally came to the vacant lot because of

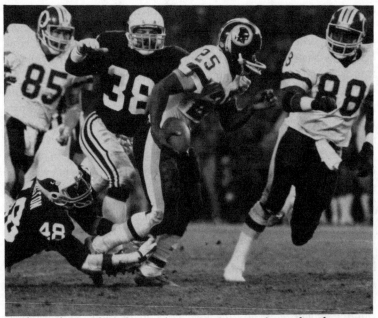

At the professional level, sport becomes an occupation rather than a pastime.

their intrinsic motivation to play softball "for the fun of it." When money was introduced into the picture as an additional reward for playing, the children began to see themselves as playing primarily to get this extrinsic reward. Once this shift in their perception of their own motives occurred, the withdrawal of the money reduced their desire to play.

Although this story is probably fictional, the principle that extrinsic rewards can undermine intrinsic motivation is not. Psychological experiments have continually shown that this can occur in children and adults alike. In youth sports there is the risk that children's intrinsic interest in the sport can be decreased if they begin to see their participation as a means to some extrinsic goals, such as trophies, trips, or state championships.

If carried to an extreme, external rewards can replace intrinsic motivation as the reason for participating in sports. When the young athletes begin to see these extrinsic rewards as the reason for their participation, the removal of these rewards may result in a loss of interest in participation.

An unhappy example of exactly this effect is the case of the teenage wrestler whose father called one of us. The father was very concerned because his young athlete refused to enter meets unless the winners' trophies were large enough to justify the effort.

We are not suggesting that trophies and other extrinsic rewards be eliminated from sports. They certainly have their rightful place as a means of recognizing outstanding effort and achievement. It is important, however, that adults and children maintain a proper perspective so that trophies do not become the be-all and end-all of participation. It is sad indeed when children lose the capacity to enjoy athletic competition for its own sake.

Sports and Character-Building

Raising our children is in large part a moral enterprise. We do our best to teach our children the difference between right and wrong. We communicate our own values to them and hope they will adopt similar values. We want them to develop positive character traits that will make them happy and contributing members of society. Our goals in this regard are shared by religious institutions, schools, youth organizations, and athletic programs. The motto of Little League Baseball—"Character, Courage, Loyalty"— exemplifies the commitment that many youth sport programs have made to develop sportsmanship and good citizenship. Adult leadership responsibilities in such programs go beyond teaching sport skills to include stressing the value of hard work, sportsmanship, and good citizenship.

"Little League Baseball has nothing to do with baseball."
H.E. Pohlman, former Little League district administrator

Not everyone agrees that youth sport programs succeed in these goals. Critics point out that in some instances impressionable youngsters learn to swear, cheat, fight, intimidate, and hurt others. Sports provide opportunities to learn immoral values and behaviors as well as moral ones. Depending on the types of leadership provided by coaches and parents, the experiences can result in sinners as well as saints. In the final analysis, it is not the sport itself that automatically determines the worth of the activity for the child, but rather the nature of the experiences within the program.

Sports are an especially promising setting for learning the positive traits we lump under the term *character*, because they confront children with many challenges that await them in later life. Cooperation, competition, perseverance in the face of difficulties, concern for others, self-sacrifice, and moral behavior (sportsmanship) can all be called for on any given day. Through the influence they have as important adults in children's lives, coaches and parents can teach children to respond to these challenges in desirable ways. Important lessons of life can be learned on the athletic field and in the gymnasium.

Many sports, particularly those that involve physical contact, require some degree of "aggressiveness" on the part of athletes. A rather fine dividing line can exist between "assertiveness," on the one hand, and "aggression," on the other. Assertiveness involves using physical force to its maximum legal limit, as when a football player makes a hard tackle. Aggression, on the other hand, is the use of physical force in a manner that is intended to hurt an opponent. Ideally, we would like our children to be appropriately assertive, but not to intentionally try to harm others.

Unfortunately, there is evidence that sports can sometimes be a "school for violence" if parents and coaches do not teach children the difference between assertiveness and aggression. A study of Canadian youth hockey players by Michael Smith of York University indicated that most of the players had learned illegal and violent tactics by watching and playing hockey. Among players who had learned illegal tactics, over 60 percent reported using the tactics themselves during the season. Moreover, even at the nine- and ten-year-old level, nearly 60 percent of the children approved of fighting, even though it is against the rules. Among older players, this increased to 84 percent. No wonder comedian Rodney Dangerfield is able to say, "I went to a fight the other night and a hockey match broke out!" Clearly, adults must be sensitive to the potential that certain "contact" sports have for teaching and rewarding aggression so that they can emphasize the importance of hard but fair play.

The Coach As Moral Philosopher

The youth sport coach is charged with teaching children not only the skills of the sport but also the value of hard work, sportsmanship, and good citizenship. To study the communication of moral values, University of Minnesota sociologist Gary Fine and his colleagues observed youth baseball coaches over a three-year period. Among the themes that the coaches stressed were effort, sportsmanship, and teamwork. Here are some examples:

> Your goal for the year is to be a winner. That doesn't mean winning every game. Sometimes you will be up against teams that are better than you. It does mean to give everything you've got. If you give everything that you've got, you're a winner in my book. The only one who cares is the Man that made you and He made both teams, both winners and losers. Give everything you've got.

Coach after his team (with a 6-3 record) loses 5-1:

> You guys are sleeping out there. If you have no pride in yourself, I don't want you . . . In other games, even in games in which you guys won, there was a lack of hustle . . . I won't quit on you, don't quit on me.

> Guys, you got a big lead—I don't want any monkeying around out there, I want no talking to them. I want you to be good sports.

Coach after come-from-behind victory:

> Isn't that nice to come back and win it? It was a team effort. Everybody played well.

In our attempts to teach children desirable attitudes and behaviors, it is important that we explain to children the principles or reasons behind desired actions. For example, rather than simply threatening to punish players for heckling opponents, a coach might help his players understand the golden rule "Do unto others as you would have them do unto you" by asking them to consider what it would be like to be the victims of heckling—and thus encourage his players to develop empathy for their opponents. This ability to place oneself in the role of another person is essential to the development of morality. Understanding and applying this golden rule can lead children to internalize the concept of sportsmanship and consideration for others.

Youngsters learn moral behavior not only through verbal explanations, rewards, and punishments but also by observing how other people behave. They imitate their parents and peers, and they model themselves after their heroes. Because coaches are often highly admired and very important in the child's life, they are especially likely to serve as models. Without realizing it, coaches can behave in ways that teach either morality or immorality. For example, by trying to get the edge by stretching the rules, coaches can easily give children the impression that cheating is not really wrong unless it is detected, and then only to the extent that it hurts the chances of winning. When coaches bend the rules in order to obtain a victory, children may conclude that the end justifies the means. Likewise, coaches who display hostility toward officials and contempt for the other team communicate the notion that such behaviors are appropriate and desirable. Even when coaches and parents preach correct values, it is essential that they themselves behave in accordance with them. Psychological experiments with children have repeatedly shown that when adults' actions are inconsistent with their words, it is the actions, not the words, that influence children's behavior. Actions do indeed speak louder than words.

In teaching moral values, what we do is as important as what we say.

Critics of youth sports sometimes attack the competitive aspect of sports as inconsistent with the development of morality and concern for others. Some, however, dispute this position, arguing that moral development is actually furthered when moral decisions come into conflict with winning. In other words, noteworthy acts of sportsmanship often involve situations in which conduct governed by a moral principle (for example, that one should not cheat) is chosen instead of victory. When a youngster makes a decision to do the right thing rather than unfairly pursue an opportunity to succeed, we have a true demonstration of moral growth. Coaches and parents are in a position to further such growth.

What, then, is the verdict on sports as a means of building character? At this point we are unable to give a definite answer, for sports are simply one aspect of the complexity of children's lives. Scientific evidence is inconclusive, although positive differences in academic achievement and personality traits are sometimes found when groups of child athletes are compared with nonathletes. A lower incidence of juvenile delinquency has consistently been found in child athletes. The difficulty has been in proving that these differences are caused by sport participation. Perhaps brighter and better-adjusted children are more likely to be attracted to sports, and that's why participation is related to these attributes. There is no denying, however, that sports are capable of furthering the character development of children if adults are able to structure sport experiences for their benefit. The sport experience is full of valuable lessons for children and can be an important training ground for moral and social development.

CHAPTER 3

CHAPTER 3
THE YOUNG ATHLETE'S BODY:
Physical Development

An athlete's body greatly affects his or her athletic potential and has much to do with the enjoyment and satisfaction that comes from training and competition. The 126-pound high school boy trying to fill out a football uniform with little more than the skin and bones of a slowly maturing adolescent cannot contribute a star performance to the team, nor is he going to remember that one of the highs of his young life was playing football. He would probably be happy to trade in his current body model for something closer to six feet in height, 180 pounds in weight, and equipped with a well-developed set of muscles.

What are the features of body structure that affect sport participation? Height is an obviously important characteristic. There is always one five-foot, eight-inch guard in a high school basketball tournament, but the six-foot, six-inch player is ten inches closer to the basket and has a better chance of scoring more points. Weight is another aspect of body size that determines potential success. The two-hundred-pound football player has a distinct playing advantage over an opponent who weighs only two-thirds as much.

Body build, or physique, must also be considered. The three major body types (somatotypes) are described as follows:

- Endomorphs are characterized by a soft roundness throughout the body, with a tendency toward fatness.

- Mesomorphs are muscular individuals with large, prominent bones.

- Ectomorphs have thin body segments and poor muscle development.

Successful athletes in a particular sport tend to have similar body builds, and their physiques are compatible with the requirements of the activity. Being a mesomorph or an ectomorph will have a lot to do with whether an individual must be satisfied with recreational jogging or will enjoy working his or her long, thin legs in competitive distance races. But having a certain body type does not guarantee success or failure. The outcome is not absolute. With this in mind, you can help your child select sports that are in harmony with his or her body build. This will give your child a better chance to achieve higher levels of performance.

In addition to body size and build, athletic performance is influenced by body composition—the relative amounts of bone, muscle, and fat that make up body mass. The role of muscle in moving the body and generating force is of prime importance. Quite simply, the more strength and power that an athlete has, the greater his or her advantage will be. On the other hand, fatty tissue represents excess baggage and is a performance-inhibitor. Fatness reduces speed, limits endurance and, in some sports, increases the risk of injury. In almost all sports, with the exception of sumo wrestling perhaps, elite athletes strive to be trim and muscular, with healthy minimal levels of body fat.

Body structure and function are important in determining how satisfying and enjoyable sports can be.

The physical characteristics that determine sport performance are constantly changing during the growing years of childhood and adolescence. Knowing something about normal growth will tell us much about what kind of athletic activity is appropriate for different ages. In other words, knowledge of the nature and extent of growth will help answer crucial questions about *what sport for what child at what age*. With such information, it is possible to project realistic expectations of sport performance on our children and to direct training programs to which their changing bodies will respond. As boys and girls move through the exciting stages of growing up in sports, some appreciation of the ever-changing body can make the experience the satisfying one it should be.

Factors That Influence Body Characteristics

With the exception of identical twins, no two human bodies are exactly the same. Body size, shape, and composition, as well as the body's million physiological characteristics, are unique to each individual. These physical traits are influenced by age and sex, along with a host of internal and external (environmental) factors. For example, the endocrine glands secrete hormones directly into the bloodstream. Hormones are basically regulators of body functions, and they play an important role in physical growth and sexual maturation. With respect to environmental forces, body structure and function depend on how adequate nutrition has been, how free from disease the body has been, and how physically active one has been.

Most importantly, body characteristics are determined by genetic factors. Certainly we know that parent height is a prime determinant of offspring height. Hereditary influences on body structure and the body's many functions are so important in determining the potential for athletic performance that it is often said that great athletes are born, not made. The significance of one's genetic endowment cannot be denied.

Aside from the size, shape, and makeup of the body, there are several ways in which body functions respond to exercise and training that are important contributors to athletic performance. As with the body's structure, these abilities to respond to training are in large part determined by genetic characteristics. They include (a) the potential for developing outstanding muscle strength, (b) the capability of producing muscle energy efficiently, and (c) the capability of increasing the body's metabolism to a very high level to meet the demands of vigorous exercise. Quick reaction and speed of movement are also important to the athlete, as are the potentials for speed and quickness. These traits are all hereditary.

If someone wishes to develop the body of an elite athlete and the potential to respond ideally to a sport training program, the individual should select his or her parents with great care.

We've emphasized that hereditary factors are critical in determining which children can look forward to being outstanding, and perhaps even elite, athletes. However, the effects of genetics are never absolute, because genes do not operate in isolation. We cannot undervalue the influence of the environments in which we live—natural and manmade.

During childhood and adolescence, regular exercise is among the many environmental factors essential to achieve full potential for growth. Moderate physical stress from the muscle activities found in most sports is generally a positive force on bone growth.

Yet it is doubtful whether training programs for young athletes have any growth-promoting effect on their height. Dramatic exercise effects do, however, occur in muscle and adipose (fat) tissue. Following the start of adolescence in males, the increase in muscle mass is directly related to the intensity and duration of training programs. And, of course, the loss of fatty tissue from exercise is a desirable effect of sport participation.

On the side of caution, relatively little is known about the limits beyond which strenuous physical activity can be harmful to a young athlete's growth. Unfortunately, there is no exact guide for determining how much activity is appropriate. The issue includes consideration of the maturation level of the child and the frequency and duration of the activity. The most reasonable approach is to rely on the child's own tolerance. The young athlete will generally know when his or her limit has been reached.

A related and equally important issue concerns the exercise tolerance of healthy children. Do endurance sports place *excessive* demands on the hearts of young athletes? No. This is a popular myth. There is increasing evidence that the growing child's heart responds favorably to physical exertion.

Children's exercise tolerance is greater than believed in the past.

The key to safely handling the demands of heavy exercise resides in the health of the child. This points to the need for careful medical screening, which includes probing for a family history of cardiac problems and any early cardiovascular difficulties. Also, in protecting the wellness of child athletes, parents cannot ignore the importance of appropriate endurance-training procedures that are supervised by competent coaches.

Patterns of Physical Growth

There is an abundance of information concerning the growth of American children. Growth can be looked at merely as heights or weights for given ages, as seen in the following figure. This type of curve (a distance curve) indicates a child's growth status, or the size attained at a particular age.

It is interesting to look at the increases in height and weight that occur during a given period of time. The velocity curve shown in the next figure illustrates the rate of growth, that is, centimeters or kilograms gained per year. We can see that the most rapid per-

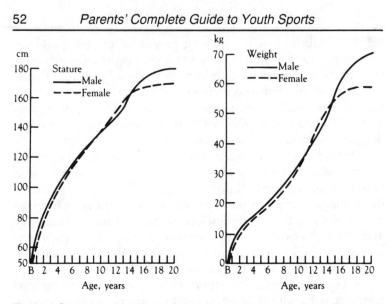

Typical Growth in Height and Weight for Boys and Girls. For Height, 2.54 cm=1 inch; for Weight, 1 kg=2.2 pounds.

iod of growth occurs immediately after birth, and then the growth rate slows to a modest, steady process during childhood. This is followed by an adolescent growth spurt and then by deceleration until growth finally stops. There is little difference in the relative growth rates of boys and girls during childhood. However, as shown in the first figure, during childhood boys are slightly taller and heavier than girls of the same age. This difference is a relatively minor one and of no real practical significance for sport performance.

When girls experience the rapid growth spurt that occurs between the ages of ten and a half and thirteen, they become taller than boys. During pubescence, tall girls will be taller than tall boys, and all girls will be taller than the shortest 3 to 5 percent of boys. This is a temporary situation that changes when boys begin to experience their adolescent growth spurt in height some two years after girls have experienced their peak velocity in gaining height.

Girls are nearer their final body size at any age because they mature at a faster rate than boys.

Prior to adolescence, sex differences in body composition are minor. However, boys do have slightly more bone and muscle tissue and less fat than girls. Following the period of maximum gain

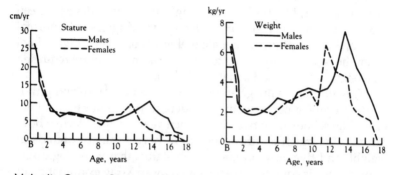

Velocity Curves Showing Rates of Increase in Height and Weight.

in height that occurs in early adolescence (about age twelve to thirteen for girls and fourteen to fifteen for boys), there is a period of maximum gain in weight. In girls this is due primarily to a large increase in body fat, with a relatively small increase in muscle tissue. In boys the rapid gain in body weight that follows a rapid gain in height is due to a decrease in body fatness and a striking increase in muscle mass. Consequently, postadolescent girls have only about two-thirds as much muscle as males, and young adult females have almost twice the amount of body fat.

Because boys on the average begin their rapid gain in height at the age of twelve and a half, they have about two more years of preadolescent growth than girls have. During this two-year period, they continue to grow, and at age fourteen or fifteen they are about four inches taller than girls were when they began their rapid growth. In the immediate preadolescent period, boys' legs grow much faster than their trunks. Thus, the longer period of preadolescent growth for males is responsible for the fact that legs of adult males are longer than those of females.

All boys and girls experience an adolescent growth spurt.

The age at which the adolescent growth spurt begins varies widely from one child to another. The variation is so great in a sample of normal males, for example, that some boys may have their most rapid growth as early as their twelfth birthday, whereas others will not have this growth experience until they are nearly sixteen. These slower-maturing boys will not have their muscle growth and rapid gain in body weight until more than fourteen months later, at seventeen or eighteen years of age. A very normal but slowly maturing young male will have completed high school before he is physically suited to compete in many sports requiring large size, strength, and a mature skeleton.

The differences in age at which adolescent growth and physical development occur are most evident during junior high school or middle school, or at twelve to fifteen years of age. Normal boys can vary as much as fifteen inches in height, ninety pounds in weight, and five years in maturation status, that is, biologic age. (Biologic age is commonly determined by an X-ray examination of skeletal maturation.) Most youth sport programs match competitors on the basis of calendar age. Therefore, large numbers of boys who do not experience their growth and maturation close to the average risk some very significant problems. This is true for both the slow later maturer and the advanced early maturer. We will discuss these specific concerns later in the chapter.

Changes in Physical Abilities During Childhood and Adolescence

During the childhood years, as boys and girls grow—resulting in longer levers and increased muscle tissue—both have the potential to increase their strength. Boys and girls show similar increased ability to perform motor skills prior to puberty. However, in general, boys are eventually able to develop greater strength and thus surpass girls in the performance of most sport-related skills.

During adolescence, males show a steady increase in performance and endurance that extends into early adulthood. The same is not true for girls. There has been a tendency for girls' performance to reach a plateau around the time of puberty (approximately thirteen years of age) and decline thereafter. Because of physical changes that accompany adolescence, such as increases in fat, girls are placed at somewhat of a disadvantage for motor performance. But the leveling off and subsequent decline in girls' performance and endurance have been related more to social factors than to biological changes.

For adolescent females, decreased motivation and increased sedentary habits are major causes of lowered performance.

Like other aspects of motor skill, strength shows a steady increase during childhood, with boys being slightly stronger than girls. Boys continue to improve during adolescence, whereas girls' strength scores level off and then tend to decrease. In boys there is a delay, on the average, of at least fourteen months between the period of the most rapid gain in height and the most rapid gain in muscle weight. The adolescent male who is nearing the completion of his rapid gain in height will have little muscle tissue and strength potential for the next year or two. He must await the development of muscles to go along with his newly acquired taller body. Thus, the adolescent male is not as strong as his stature might suggest.

This lag in strength was apparent in a seven-foot, two-inch basketball freshman at the University of Georgia who had not yet begun his muscle maturation and weight gain. At seven-two he weighed only 172 pounds. When he suffered a muscle strain, his coach remarked, "This is good news and bad news. The bad news is that he is going to miss practice for several days. The good news is that now we know he has a muscle."

Research on strength development of boys under fourteen in training programs is not extensive. The best information available indicates that prior to this age (and the production of the male sex hormone testosterone), weight training cannot be expected to result in any worthwhile gains in either muscle development or strength. In addition, weight training for preadolescent boys is an activity with high injury risk if not properly supervised.

Because the increase in weight of the adolescent female is due primarily to a gain in fat (and, to only a small extent, to a gain in muscle), her potential for strength development via exercise is much less than the male's. The extent to which girls' smaller amount of muscle tissue can be increased and strength gained by weight training has not been systematically studied. In young adult women, weight training has been shown to produce significant gains in strength, but in the absence of male hormones, the female will experience minimal gains in the size and mass of muscles.

Should Boys and Girls Compete Against Each Other?

We have pointed out that during childhood years, only very slight sex differences in body structure and motor performance are present. On a purely physical basis, there is no reason why boys and girls should not be on the same teams competing with and against each other. The potential for performance and the chances for causing or sustaining injury related to size and strength do not differ significantly between the two sexes.

However, this situation changes drastically during adolescence. As boys gain more in height, weight, muscle mass, and strength, it is not possible for girls to fairly and safely compete against them in most sports.

After puberty, girls should have separate but equal opportunities for sport participation.

There is little merit to the argument that if a girl is good enough, she should be allowed to compete on the boys' team. If one accepts this position, then boys who are good enough should be allowed to play on girls' teams. Boys would occupy most of the places on both teams because of their greater size and strength, and almost all girls would be denied places on either team. After age eleven, boys and girls should have their own competitive opportunities in those sports in which strength and body size are determinants of proficiency and injury risk.

Whether boys and girls should compete against one another depends on the sport and the age of the children.

The Growing and Maturing Skeleton

The body skeleton is obviously involved in the normal growth of children. In adolescents the skeleton first grows in size and length, after which it gains in density and strength. As mentioned earlier, the principal sites of growth before the start of rapid adolescent growth are in the legs and arms. During the adolescent growth spurt, the trunk grows most rapidly. The long bones of the arms and legs increase their length by the activity of specialized cells located in a so-called growth plate at either end of the shaft of the long bones.

Because it is composed of cartilage (soft tissue), the growth plate is structurally the weakest point in the bone. It is weaker than any point in the shaft of the bone and actually weaker than the ligaments that align the neighboring joints. Additionally, the growth plate is weakest during periods of most rapid growth. Injury to this area of the bone can destroy those cells responsible for the future growth of the long bone. During the period of the most rapid gain in height (on the average, ages fourteen to fifteen in boys and twelve to thirteen in girls), severe injury to the ends of long bones can threaten the growth plate. Growth arrest and a shortened leg could result in lifelong crippling if a long bone of the leg is involved.

The growth plate of the young athlete is vulnerable to injury.

Fortunately, growth-plate injuries are not common in sports. But the threat of a growth-plate injury would temporarily direct early adolescents away from participation in collision sports, such as football and wrestling, where severe blows to a leg or arm may be encountered. As growth nears completion in later adolescence, the growth plate ceases its function, fuses firmly with the shaft of the long bone, and is no longer the site of vulnerability that it was during early adolescence.

As the skeleton matures, the bones become denser, stronger, and more able to withstand the trauma of hard use in intensive training. There is little information on the effects on the skeleton of intense, repeated athletic activity during childhood and very early adolescence. In the absence of well-documented research, it is wise to follow the recommendations of such concerned organizations as the American Academy of Pediatrics' Sports Medicine Committee, which discourages intense athletic activities, such as long-distance running and weight training, during childhood and until the rapid growth of early adolescence has been completed.

Sport Participation and Physical Maturity

We have mentioned that body structure and a variety of basic functions that relate to athletic performance undergo striking change during the early years of adolescence. And there is great variation in the age at which individuals experience these changes. Therefore, the age at which children (boys in particular) are physically ready for many types of sports will also vary greatly. Youth sport programs present the early adolescent (junior high or middle school-aged person) with opportunities for highly organized sports. It thus becomes important to identify late-maturing and early-maturing individuals if they are to be directed into appropriate sport experiences. The late maturer will have increased risk of injury, with his undeveloped muscles and immature skeleton. More importantly, playing with and competing against larger, stronger, and more mature boys, the late maturer will be a less-skilled athlete. He is a prime candidate to drop out at the earliest opportunity.

The considerable variation in the onset of physical development at adolescence raises the question of the appropriateness of collision sports for junior high school and middle school boys. After one junior high school football game, twenty-two players were weighed. They varied in weight from 84 to 212 pounds. Although the players' physical maturity was not scientifically assessed, the range of maturity seemed also to be extremely varied—as much as four or five years' variation in skeletal maturity. Unless rather elaborate steps are taken to match competitors on the basis of maturity and size in football, wrestling, and ice hockey, it is difficult to justify these sports for middle and junior high school programs.

The Early Maturer

The early-maturing individual is bigger, stronger, and quicker, acquires sport skills faster, and has more endurance potential than his peers. Thus, the early-maturing boy can be expected to be a star grade school and junior high school athlete.

That early-maturing boys excel in several juvenile athletic programs has been well documented. In football and track-and-field events, early maturity has been shown to be a prime determinant of proficiency. Players at the Little League World Series have been studied using bone-age X-rays to document their maturation sta-

Children competing at the same level may differ greatly in physical maturity.

tus. Seventy-one percent of these twelve-year-old star athletes had advanced bone ages. Those with the most advanced bone age were pitchers, first basemen, left fielders, and those who batted fourth (clean-up) in the batting lineup. In the 1982 World Series, the winning pitcher in the championship game was a very mature five-foot, eight-inch, 174-pound twelve-year-old.

The difference in ability level of young athletes is often a result of different maturity levels.

A major problem is that the early maturer enjoys outstanding sport success during elementary, middle, and early junior high school simply because of the physical advantages he has over his teammates and opponents. With the elaborate sport programs available for very young athletes in most communities, the eight-to twelve-year-old can readily become a true sports star. That winning Little League pitcher mentioned above was flown to New York from the West Coast to appear on a national prime-time television show, and he was given a page and a half write-up in

Sports Illustrated. A local television commentator suggested that the junior high school where he had just started seventh grade be named after him. Pretty heady stuff for a twelve-year-old.

The sport success of an early-maturing boy can lead to a full-time commitment to one or more sports at a very early age. Sport achievements may eliminate the desire for accomplishment in other areas, such as schoolwork or the arts, or an interest in exploring other sports. Positive reinforcements come from coaches, teammates, and most particularly parents, who sometimes begin to think of their star athlete in terms of outstanding high school performances, college scholarships, and perhaps even a high-salaried career in professional sports. What does it matter if the only musical instrument the child will ever be interested in playing is a tape deck or that his report card is full of C's and D's?

The world can fall apart for this youngster and his family about high school time, when as a sophomore he lines up against some juniors and seniors who possess his same maturity. Having lost the advantage of his early development, the young man is now less than an outstanding athlete. As all of his former grade school teammates and opponents catch up to him in maturity and as other athletes begin to do outstanding things, the grade school star may find only an uncomfortable place on the bench. Unable to understand the true reason that the star no longer outshines others, insensitive coaches and even parents may accuse him of "dogging it." The young man has lost the limelight of sport success on which his self-esteem was built. He is left with no other interests or talents because of his early all-consuming commitment to the sport, and he is keenly aware of the great disappointment he is to his parents. At sixteen or seventeen, an age of considerable vulnerability to a number of disturbing antisocial alternatives, he is a depressed has-been.

**The potential problems of early-maturing athletes
are fairly easy to avoid.**

The answer, of course, is to prevent the problems from occurring. This can be done by first recognizing the signs of early maturity. The early maturer will probably be the son of a father who likewise was an early maturer, and he will experience growth changes and sexual maturation well ahead of schedule. Once identified as an individual who is maturing more rapidly than usual, he should have the opportunity to participate in sports with individuals who are of similar maturity, not the same calendar age. The early-maturing star basketball player of junior high school should have a chance to work out with the high school junior varsity. Matches can be arranged for the twelve-year-old tennis star with some sixteen-year-old members at the tennis club. Early-maturing boys need to know how really good they are if they are to keep their athletic performances and potentials in proper perspective.

The Late Maturer

With sport successes so closely related to maturity, it isn't difficult to imagine the problems of the late-maturing boy—especially for parents who were late maturers themselves. Many, but certainly not all, late maturers will be small in stature for their age. They will have less strength, endurance, and skeletal maturity and lower motor skills than their average peers. These boys are going to be handicapped in many sports where size, strength, and endurance determine the outcome, and in some situations they will be at undue risk to injury.

The late-maturing individual will often be recognized as such in his elementary school years. A father's own maturation experience from twelve to sixteen years of age can be an indicator of the maturation rate to be expected of the son. If early sport participation is important for the late maturer, he should be directed to sports that are not primarily dependent on size and strength for proficiency, such as racket sports, diving, and some track events. He may not become state champion, but he may achieve levels of accomplishment sufficient to earn him a comfortable place in the sport scene.

Many late maturers can comfortably postpone their entry into sport programs until they are physically mature. Club activities, scouting, music, and other activities may satisfy in the meanwhile. It is most important that these boys know the normal sequence of changes that occur during adolescence so that they know where they are in the maturation process, where they are going, and when they get there. With this insight they will know when sports can be rewarding, when a vigorous training program can be effective and satisfying, and when they can be competitive on the field or court. It is possible at ages fourteen to sixteen to avoid a devastating, negative sport experience due to delayed maturity. The late maturer doesn't have to suffer consistent setbacks and be turned off to sports and their benefits.

**Late-maturing youngsters need understanding and
special attention from parents and coaches.**

Parents and coaches should know the implications of delayed adolescent development in these boys, and they should develop their expectations accordingly. Limited training for strength and endurance during the first two years of high school should be accompanied by large doses of encouragement at home and on the court or field. Properly managed, the late maturer can be a budding sport star by the senior year of high school. Being constantly yelled at by a coach or put down by a disappointed parent can produce a demoralized dropout at an age when dropping out can be very serious.

The Body of Today's Young Athlete

Those responsible for sport programs for children and youth must recognize that athletes are a different population from those of a generation or two ago. Athletes today are bigger and stronger at younger ages. Particularly at the junior and senior high school levels, the "new model" athletes not only perform better, they demand a higher degree of sophistication and concern in dealing with their protective equipment, training facilities, coaching, refereeing, and even rule changes.

**Children are growing to a larger size and maturing
more rapidly than ever before.**

The young athlete's body is the prime determinant of proficiency and satisfaction in sports. Since physical features are constantly changing during childhood and adolescence, sport programs and expectations must be adjusted according to these developmental changes. From a purely physical viewpoint, the sport programs of elementary school children must minimize demands for strength and endurance. The potential for developing these traits is not present at this age. Prior to the age of twelve or thirteen, sports should be for fun, for experiencing a variety of opportunities, and for being introduced to some sport skills.

During those rapidly changing years from twelve to sixteen, with their tremendous variation in adolescent body changes, more attention should be paid to the proper matching of competitors.

Young athletes should ideally be of a similar maturational level regardless of their calendar ages. Sports provide a critical opportunity to acquire much-needed confidence in oneself and in one's newly developed physique. The adolescent should not be denied this opportunity or have a negative experience because of inappropriate matching or the unrealistic expectations of parents and coaches.

CHAPTER 4

CHAPTER 4
CHOOSING A SPORT PROGRAM:
A First Step to a Good Experience

Betty had a lot of potential. She was tall, strong, and well coordinated for her age. She also had a strong competitive spirit and a genuine interest in gymnastics. But that's all gone now.

Because of Betty's interest in gymnastics, her parents enrolled her in an athletic club near her home. Although the facility was excellent, the program left a lot to be desired from both a medical and a psychological point of view. The coach was a hard-driving man who demanded total dedication from youngsters. "Dedication" was instilled by threats that those who did not develop fast enough would not be entered in meets. Daily practices were pressured and exhausting. There was no time for friends or other activities. Like some of the other gymnasts, Betty was put on a highly restrictive diet without medical consultation. At one point the coach suggested that she take illegal steroids to increase her strength and muscle mass. His constant prodding that she attempt more dangerous routines resulted in repeated injuries. After a year in the club, Betty completely burned out. She dropped out of gymnastics and vowed never to have anything to do with the sport again.

Pete's story is different. His mother and father were divorced when he was very young. Because his mother was forced to work, he had little parental guidance. As early as the second grade, Pete began to have conduct problems in school. A few years later he became involved with a youth gang and ended up under arrest for shoplifting. He seemed well on his way to a life of delinquency. Pete's life turned around when his mother enrolled him in the local YMCA, where he came under the influence of a young supervisor who steered him into the Youth Basketball Association league. Here Pete found a constructive outlet for his energies, and he developed a sense of belonging. His mother's work schedule allowed her to attend his games, and he felt great pride in being part of the team. His conduct problems in school disappeared, and he began to apply himself to his schoolwork just as he had to basketball.

Pete's story has a happy ending, whereas Betty's is tragic. One youngster found fulfillment in a sport program. The other was turned off as a result of a bad experience. Their stories illustrate the importance of selecting a good program.

Most children enter sport programs more or less through chance. Often a parent knows relatively little about a program, its philosophy, or the nature of the leadership provided. For most children, entering a program is a matter of doing what one's friends are doing or it is a matter of practical factors, such as its location and availability.

But there is much to be said for parental involvement and guidance at even this first stage of selecting a program. Youngsters can't be expected to critically evaluate a particular program. They need the assistance of their parents. If an appropriate program is selected, many unnecessary difficulties and problems can be avoided. Therefore, we strongly recommend that you take the time and effort to arrive at a well-informed choice.

Your Responsibility as a Parent

Parents have both the right and the responsibility to inquire about *all* activities that their children are involved in, including sports. You should take this responsibility seriously, probing into the nature and the quality of specific sport programs. By so doing, you are not being overly protective or showing a lack of confidence in a program. Rather, you are fulfilling a child-rearing obligation to oversee the welfare of your loved one.

It is important that you gather the information necessary to make the right decision for you and for your child.

Inquiries by parents, if made appropriately, should be welcomed by sport-program directors and coaches. They, like you, should have as their major concern the welfare of your child. If your inquiries are not welcomed or even responded to, you have cause for concern about the program.

Deciding Together

Selection of a program should be a joint decision of parent and child. Although you have the final say in the matter, it is important to involve your child in the decision-making process, taking into account very seriously what your child wants to get out of the sport experience. It is a mistake for parents to assume that they know what a child wants without asking him or her. A parent whose goal is for the youngster to excel as an athlete might choose a different program than one who takes into account simply the child's desire to participate with his or her friends. A direct discussion in which you share your own experiences and opinions with your youngster rather than force them on him or her is the best approach.

Children should not be rushed into competition at too early an age.

Because all programs are run by human beings, you should not expect to find a fault-free program. Most have certain flaws, but this does not mean that the entire experience will be a bad one for your child. If you make a commitment to work with, not against, a program, you may be able to help correct any shortcomings.

How Early Should Children Participate?

This is not an easy question to answer. Children differ a great deal in their maturity, their aspirations, and their abilities. For these reasons, it is impossible to recommend a specific age for participation of all children in all sports. In the final analysis, it depends on your child's characteristics, the sport in question, and the nature of the program. Children should not be rushed into organized athletics; they need time to enjoy free play with their friends, for much development occurs in such play. Certainly one important indicator of readiness is the child's own expression of interest in participating. But parents and coaches must fall back on common sense to make a decision in a particular case.

The best guide is to know the child, the sport, and the program.

Based on available scientific and medical evidence, and taking into account individual differences in physical and psychological readiness to compete, we recommend the following age guidelines:

Noncontact sports (baseball, swimming, track, tennis):	6-8 years
Contact sports (soccer, basketball, wrestling):	8-10 years
Collision sports (tackle football, hockey):	10-12 years

Which Sports Should Your Child Play?

Again, the answer to this question depends basically on your youngster's interests. There are additional factors to be taken into account, however. Such factors as safety, the benefits of individual versus team sports, and the season of the year may all influence decisions. You may be perfectly happy to have your child play outdoor soccer during warm months, but have health concerns about the same sport during cold winter months.

Parents frequently inquire about the benefits of individual versus team sports. Again, there is no simple answer to this question and no reliable scientific research to help guide decisions. However, one can make some broad and general comparisons. On the whole, team sports provide more opportunities for learning social skills and making friends. There is also more need for cooperation and more emphasis placed on willingness to sacrifice personal interests for the good of the team. More opportunities exist in team sports to specialize and find a niche suited to personal interests and abilities. A youngster with a poor throwing arm can play first base in baseball, and a big youngster with a poor shooting touch can become a rebounding terror in basketball. On the other hand, a youngster in an individual sport, such as tennis, needs to be able to master all the skills of the sport. Finally, it is often the case that team sports generate more camaraderie, or "we" feelings, than do individual sports. Many youngsters are attracted to the sense of belonging that exists in team sports.

Individual sports generally require more self-sufficiency. The athlete cannot rely on anyone else to get the job done. Competition takes the form of one-on-one duels, and success or failure is shouldered solely by the individual. There is less of the social support that is provided by teammates in team sports. This can foster a strong sense of personal responsibility and independence. Because of these factors, individual sports tend to be more intensely competitive at a personal level and often demand more in the way of "mental toughness." Also, more personal dedication is often required of the athlete in training.

"Boxing should be banned, forbidden, and eliminated forever as a sport for children."
Rainer Martens, sport psychologist and youth sport authority

We feel that almost all sports have something to offer children. However, we do have major reservations about boxing. Boxing is the only sport whose goal is to harm another person. Reports of twelve-year-old amateur boxers who have registered strings of knockouts are chilling reminders of the basic brutality of the sport. Although we acknowledge the fact that some underprivileged youths have found social and economic salvation through boxing, we do not believe that boxing in itself offers any benefits that cannot be achieved through other, less dangerous sports.

How Many Sports Should Your Child Play?

No matter how enjoyable or fulfilling sport participation is, it does take time and divert attention from other activities. For most children, one sport at a time is plenty during the school year. The time and energy demands on both children and their parents need to be kept at a reasonable level.

During the summer months, multiple-sport participation seems more reasonable. A child may have enough time and energy to be involved in several sports, such as baseball, tennis, and swimming.

Sometimes the best decision is not to participate. Participation in sports, although desirable, is not necessarily for everyone. Parents should not feel that their child must be on a team or involved in a sport. For those children who wish to direct their energies in other ways, the best program may be no program. Many parents become unnecessarily alarmed if their child does not show an interest in sports. They think that a child who would rather do other things must somehow be abnormal. Forcing a child into sports against his or her will can be a big mistake. Sometimes the wisest decision is to encourage the child to move into other activities that may be more suited to his or her interests and abilities, at least until an interest in sports develops.

Sources of Information and How to Get It

Many programs have preseason meetings to provide parents with information and to answer their questions. Such meetings can also serve as forums for parents to give input regarding concerns, opinions, and suggestions. When you attend a meeting of this kind, look for openness on the part of administrators. They should show a willingness to exchange information with the intent of promoting greater understanding and cooperation. If a program does not have such a meeting, you might suggest it to the administrator and perhaps volunteer to assist in its organization.

A preseason sport orientation meeting is a good investment for everyone.

If a preseason meeting is not scheduled for parents, you may have to obtain information directly from the program administrators or coaches. It is well to make up a list of questions and concerns before speaking with them. In dealing with program leaders, remember that they are volunteering their time and effort for the benefit of children who participate in their program. They deserve courtesy and your respect!

Another very useful source of information about a program is parents of youngsters who have been through it. They can provide firsthand and candid feedback concerning the merits and shortcomings of the program. As consumers of the program, they may be in the best position to evaluate it for you.

Some Important Considerations in Deciding on a Program

Eventually the decision will come down to whether or not to join a particular program. Sometimes you might be choosing among several alternatives, such as the church-sponsored basketball league, the one sponsored by your local parks department, or the one at the junior high. At other times there may be only one program available, and your decision will be based on whether it meets your child's needs and whether the costs or possible physical risks involved are balanced by the benefits. In either of these cases, there are some key points about sport programs that you should keep in mind to help guide your decision.

Organization and Administration

The success of any program depends on how it is run and who is running it. You should make it a point to find out whether the program is administered by one person or by a board of directors (which is likely to include a wider range of viewpoints and representation). Of crucial importance is the extent to which you as a parent can have an influence on decisions that will affect your child.

Potential problems can occur when a program is run by a small clique that is not open to input from parents.

Programs also vary in how much information they give parents about policies and practices. Parents should be given an account of how revenues are spent to benefit children. Two key questions to ask are whether board meetings are held and if parents are welcome to attend. Some very effective programs welcome involvement by parents in a variety of ways and organize social events in which parents can interact with their children.

Costs and Commitments

It's rare in this world to get something for nothing. Most programs require commitments of time and money. It's wise for parents to know the costs sooner rather than later. The costs can be financial/entry fees, equipment, uniforms, transportation for trips, contributions to fund-raisers, and so forth. In sports such as tennis, gymnastics, and figure skating, these costs can multiply rapidly in the form of private lessons and coaching, racket- or skating-club fees, and trips to distant meets. Many parents have found themselves in over their heads financially and unable to pull back because the child has become involved beyond the point of no return. It's a good idea to ask parents who are already in the program for information.

Other costs may be in terms of time and emotional involvement. You can easily get into a program for your child's sake (or for your own hoped-for peace and quiet) only to find yourself stuck in a quicksand of time commitments. Suddenly you're spending hours driving to games and practices, manning the hot dog booth, and going door-to-door selling candy bars. Those glorious days of working in the garden or watching the weekend ballgames on TV are now a thing of the past.

Now, you may well make the choice to be time-involved, but to make an informed decision, you should try to find out:

- How many practices and games per week are there?
- Where are they held?
- Who provides transportation?
- Is there car pooling?
- What responsibilities are expected of parents? For example, are they expected to organize fund-raisers or to participate in field maintenance?
- Are allowances made for family vacations during the season, or will your family's vacation have to be postponed or canceled?
- Will your child have time for other activities? Obviously, if practices are held every night for two hours, there will be little time for other pursuits.

- Do practices and game schedules interfere with
  dinner time, homework, church or Sunday school, or
  family outings?

- How long does the season last? In warm climates
  youth baseball tryouts can begin as early as January,
  making for a far longer season than in snowbound
  regions.

Program Philosophy and Objectives

The philosophy and values underlying a program can mean
the difference between a positive experience and a negative one for
your child. These values influence the goals that are set and the
approaches used to pursue them. In Chapter 1 we stressed the crucial differences between the professional model and the developmental model of sports. It is important to keep these differences in
mind as you examine a program.

**The professional sport model operates on the
premise that winning is everything, whereas the
developmental model insists that kids are
everything.**

Although we believe that the psychological and physical welfare of child athletes is best served in programs that emphasize participation, fun, and personal growth, we also recognize that some
parents and children prefer win-oriented programs, even at very
early ages. At the high school level, virtually all programs emphasize athletic excellence and winning. It is a parent's right to choose
such a program, but it is also the parent's responsibility to make
sure that winning is not emphasized to the exclusion of the young
athlete's interests. Many cases of athletic burnout result from pressures created by program philosophies that place winning first and
athletes second.

Some national programs emphasize their underlying philosophy very directly. Little League Baseball, Pony Baseball, the
AAU/USA Junior Olympics, the American Youth Soccer Association, the YWCA and YMCA, the Catholic Youth Organization, and
the American Junior Bowling Congress are among those whose
philosophies emphasize personal growth through sports. However, at a local level even these programs can vary in their commitment to the principles of the larger organization. Therefore, it is
important to examine each program on an individual basis and to
talk with parents whose children have been in the programs.

In examining a particular program, you may wish to get answers to the following questions:

- Does the program have a written statement of its goals and philosophy that is available to parents? If so, are they consistent with your needs?

- Is participation for everyone emphasized? Do all youngsters who turn out get a chance to play? Do some players get cut? Are there rules requiring that all children on a team get a certain amount of playing time?

- Is competition kept in perspective? Is competition seen as deadly serious business or as a contest in which to have fun? Are players taught to regard their opponents as enemies or as friendly challengers who make the contest possible?

- Are the needs of athletes taken into account in making decisions about such things as the time and length of practices and games? Are there attempts to match teams on the basis of size and ability for safe and equal competition?

- Are youngsters treated fairly? Do all children receive attention and instruction, or only the best performers? Is the emphasis on giving every child a good experience or on developing a select group of gifted athletes for higher levels of competition?

- Are attempts made to teach children sportsmanship and moral values? Is social and emotional development promoted?

- Are the rewards of participation viewed in terms of personal and team improvement or in the form of trophies, victory banquets, and all-star teams? Is the most improved athlete as important to the program as the most valuable athlete?

Program Safety

The physical well-being of your youngster is surely of concern in choosing a program. There will always be injuries in sports, but a safety-conscious program can help keep the risks at a minimum.

Many programs are emphasizing the desirability of a medical examination prior to participating, and some programs are requiring it. Children who have a physical condition that places them at high risk can often be identified and saved from injury. Several medical studies have shown preparticipation physical examinations to be associated with a lower rate of serious injuries.

Recognizing the value of screening examinations, some programs have contracted with sports medicine clinics or with individual physicians to make the exams less costly for parents. It is wise to inquire about this when selecting a program.

The safety of participants is increased when a program has developed safety rules for practices and games and when such rules are strictly enforced. Playing areas should be kept safe and free from hazards, such as holes, rocks, and broken glass. Your inquiry into these matters helps to draw necessary attention to them.

Try as we might to prevent them, injuries will occur and occasionally they will be serious ones. It is therefore important that coaches or adult supervisors who are trained in first aid be present at practices and games. There should also be established procedures in the event of an emergency.

Safety-conscious programs have leaders who are prepared to deal quickly and effectively with injuries and emergencies when they occur.

Everyone is aware of the rising costs of health care and the resulting need to have insurance protection. Some programs require accident insurance for all participants. Several insurance groups offer athletic accident insurance to youth sport programs at reasonable rates. You should inquire about such coverage when considering a program. If the program does not subscribe to injury insurance, be certain that your own insurance provides adequate coverage for sport-related injuries to your youngster.

The likelihood of injuries increases when participants vary greatly in size, strength, and maturity. It is the smaller, less-developed player who is at greater risk under such circumstances. Research has shown that injuries can be reduced in collision sports, such as football or hockey, by matching participants in terms of size rather than by relying simply on age. Such matching not only reduces injuries but also gives all participants a greater opportunity to enjoy success and fair competition.

Quality of Leadership

When all is said and done, the most important factor of all in determining the outcome of your child's experience is the quality of adult supervision in the program you choose. The relationship that develops between your youngster and the coach or manager can become a very important one in your child's life. This adult will not only teach your child the techniques of the sport, but will also create a psychological climate that can have long-term effects. Coaches communicate important attitudes and values, and they serve as role models for children at an impressionable time in their lives.

Anytime you place your child in the hands of another adult, you should have confidence that he or she has what it takes to shoulder the responsibilities. Remember, most youth sport programs are staffed by volunteers who are sincerely interested in children. But this interest must be accompanied by knowledge of the sport and of a child's needs.

The most effective coaches are not only good teachers but good amateur psychologists as well.

Many programs now recognize that they have a responsibility to prepare coaches for their leadership role. They also realize that instruction in the technical aspects of the sport is not enough. Workshops and clinics should focus on how to create a good psychological environment for personal and social growth and how to promote the physical safety of participants. Selection of a program for your youngster should thus be based in part on how well coaches are trained and evaluated. No matter what the program's potential may be, a subpar coach can ruin an otherwise good experience.

Before the season begins and while you're looking into a program, you may not know much about who will be coaching your youngster. At this point, about all you can do is to ask whether the coaches have preseason training or have gone through a certification program. Once the season begins, however, you will have opportunities to observe the coach. This is your right and your responsibility.

What should you look for in a coach? Here is a short checklist of qualities that we believe are important in a youth sport coach.

Knowledge and Teaching Skills

- Does the coach know the rules and techniques of the sport? Can he communicate these to children?

- Does he or she demonstrate how to perform, and does he or she give clear explanations?

- Are practices and games well organized, safe, and fun for the children?

- Is instruction matched to the age and knowledge level of the children? Or is the coach trying to run a Dallas Cowboys multiple offense with a team of eight-year-olds, who are probably not yet certain whether the face mask faces front or back?

Motives and Philosophy

- Does the coach seem to have a sincere interest in youngsters, or is coaching an ego trip?

- Does the coach put winning and losing in perspective? Is the focus where it should be—on fun, participation for all, and learning?

- Does the coach teach values as well as skills?

- Can the coach communicate his or her coaching philosophy to athletes and parents?

Coaching Style

- Does the coach try to motivate athletes through encouragement and praise, or do punishment and criticism dominate?

- Does the coach seem enthusiastic and enjoy relating to the athletes? Does the coach have fun?

- Are substitutes given as much attention as the stars, or are they ignored and made to feel unimportant?

- Does the coach keep things well organized and prevent misbehavior, or does he or she let things get out of hand and have to scold the children to maintain control?

- Does the coach recognize and praise good effort even when things are not going well?

- Does the coach ask for input from athletes and listen to it, or does he or she call all the shots?

- Can the coach control his or her own emotions, or does the coach lose his or her cool with athletes or officials and provide a poor role model?

Relationship Skills

- Is the coach sensitive to the individual needs and feelings of the athletes?

- Can the coach be flexible and know when everybody should *not* be treated exactly alike?

- Can the coach generate respect without demanding it and show respect for athletes, officials, and opponents?

- Is the coach fair and consistent in his or her expectations of athletes?

- Can the coach communicate effectively with youngsters at their level?

- Do athletes he or she has coached wish to play for him or her again?

- Does the coach take the time and effort to communicate with parents, and is he or she open to their input?

Obviously no sport program is going to be perfect, since all are run by fallible human beings. You can't expect to get answers to every question presented here. But weighing the pros and cons can help you increase the chances of selecting the best program for your youngster and starting your young athlete on the road to a good sport experience.

CHAPTER 5

CHAPTER 5
FOOD FOR SPORT:
Nutrition Tips for Young Athletes

Few things regularly raise more questions in the minds of parents of young athletes than concerns about how and what they should eat. As Mom wonders whether or not the children are really getting a balanced diet, Dad knows that if Carla or Brian would only eat better, she or he surely would play better. The professional nutritionist says that all the athlete needs is a generous balanced diet; the media tell about the professional tennis star who takes hundreds of food-supplement pills each day. Whom do you listen to? How does one best satisfy the nutritional needs of active young competitors? Nothing less than optimal nutrition will be acceptable to highly competitive athletes. They know that their diet does indeed have something important to do with performance in sports.

Unique Nutrition Needs of the Young Athlete

Active, energy-expending sport participation creates two and only two unique nutritional requirements: (a) a need for increased food-energy intake to meet the needs of training and competition, and (b) an increased demand for water intake to replace the sweat lost during exercise. Satisfying these needs is essential for good performance as well as for the health and safety of the athlete. In addition, the young preadolescent and the older adolescent athlete have important growth needs that must be met.

Eating satisfies four vital needs. These are especially important for the growing youngster and take on additional importance for the physically active participant in sports. Eating:

- Provides energy
- Supplies chemical building blocks for growth and repair of body tissues

- Supplies essential chemicals needed for a host of body functions
- Satisfies important psychosocial needs through interaction with family and friends during mealtime

Living in a food-excess society, the vast majority of American young people have food available in abundance to satisfy the first three needs. National nutrition surveys find little evidence of any lack of specific nutrients in the diets of most Americans. Between 85 and 90 percent of the citizens of the United States have access to enough food to satisfy their energy needs and the nutritional needs for normal growth. The other 10 to 15 percent of citizens, who live in poverty, do not have access to adequate diets—a problem of continuing importance and concern to all of us.

The fourth need, to satisfy social and behavioral requirements that are met through the eating process, is of increasing concern. Loss of mealtime patterns, the changing family composition, and changing life styles all raise questions as to whether young people, even in our food-abundant environment, are getting an adequate diet and the security, education, and learning experiences that come from mealtime contact with family and friends.

The quality of the diet is directly proportionate to the quality of the environment in which the food is eaten.

For almost all Americans, eating in a pleasant place with amiable people essentially guarantees that the nutritional quality of their diet will be very high and more than adequate. (One would like to always believe that the most pleasant place and most amiable people would be at the family table.) Eating alone or on the run is the surest way to eat badly. Unfortunately, too many young athletes and families eat this way.

The Young Athlete's Diet

Parents are keenly aware that the elementary school-aged child has to eat right to grow right, but a new dimension of food need has been introduced into the parenting concerns of many families: how to feed a growing boy or girl who is now an athlete. In previous chapters, the goals of good sport participation have been clearly spelled out—having fun, getting some exercise, learning skills, and becoming familiar with sports. These goals are in no way in conflict with the goals of good nutrition for young athletes.

Actually, attempting to exploit new sport interests of boys and girls to get them to eat more or differently can jeopardize the most important goal of youth sport participation—to have fun. The ten-year-old athlete shouldn't be cajoled into eating three health-promoting meals a day simply to make him a better quarterback, second baseman, or figure skater. He or she should have an opportunity to eat those three health-promoting and pleasant meals to make him or her the most fit ten-year-old. Sport interests should not be used as a weapon at mealtime. It is the parents' responsibility to provide a desirable selection of menu items at mealtime.

Concerned parents determine *what* the young athlete will eat. Nature will direct the young athlete as to *how much* to eat.

Youth sport participation by the preadolescent should not be such an intense experience that satisfying excessive energy expenditures is a concern. However, monitoring water needs during practice and competition is becoming an increasing problem as very young athletes become more active in intensely competitive situations where temperature and humidity are high. The specific needs and hazards of fluid replacement in athletes will be considered later in this chapter. It is a common problem in the more intense activities of older athletes, but there is now a very real need to be alert to the fluid requirements of the elementary school-aged athlete as well.

How Sports Can Interfere with Good Nutrition

Can youth sport participation interfere with the good nutrition and good growth that result from healthy eating during childhood? "With a girl in gymnastics and two boys in soccer and baseball," said one parent, "mealtime eating together is a matter of historical interest in our family."

We sincerely believe that a good sport experience contributes to growing up healthy in today's society. Yet we recognize that there are other needs, priorities, and growth-promoting requirements of a happy, healthy childhood. Yes, there is life beyond sports! Before family life and mealtime disappear from your household, we suggest that you hold a family council with the children, define the goals of youth sports, and then preserve a generous number of those valuable weekends, mealtimes, and other times for being together as a family.

It is equally important to be alert to the impact of more intense, competitive sport participation on the dietary needs of the adolescent athlete during his or her high school and early college years.

Scott was sent to a sports medicine clinic because of a rather rapid deterioration in performance with his high school swim team. It was early in the preseason, and already Scott seemed to be "stale." He had no specific complaints that suggested he might be ill, but he did state that he had lost between eleven and thirteen pounds during the first two months of training. His grades in school were great—straight A's—but he was getting very worried about his swim performance.

Scott was a good swimmer—state high school champion last year and ranked nationally this year. He had decided to take this year to find out just how good he could be. He was swimming up to 20,000 meters a day (about twelve miles), doing his academic work, and volunteering two evenings a week as a clerk in a storefront health clinic. He "usually" ate lunch, seldom ate breakfast, and "got dinner somewhere" every evening. Although a very intelligent young man, Scott couldn't (or wouldn't) understand why he was losing weight and underperforming. The fact was that his food-energy intake was simply inadequate to meet the very generous energy expenditures of his active lifestyle and extremely demanding training schedule.

Food-energy intake insufficient to satisfy the demands of growth, training, and daily school activities is the most common nutrition-related problem encountered among young athletes. Like Scott, many athletes become overcommitted to an extent that their lifestyles allow no time for eating. Others come from disorganized families in which food is not regularly available or from impoverished homes in which there is no adequate food supply. Whatever the reason might be, when energy intake is inadequate to meet the needs of the active young male or female athlete, there will be involuntary weight loss. And it is inevitable that the athlete will experience a deterioration in performance. Recorded weighing once or twice each week will identify the athlete whose diet is inadequate to meet energy needs.

**Maintaining a stable desired weight assures that
food energy intakes are sufficient to satisfy energy
demands.**

Two groups of athletes most likely to experience involuntary weight loss and poor training performance are swimmers and basketball players. These high-energy-expending individuals may find that three meals a day plus a generous evening snack are not enough to satisfy their energy needs. If a larger diet does not stabilize competing weight during the season and if adding extra meals or snacks is unacceptable to the athlete in question, the use of a convenient liquid food can be helpful by providing 500 to 1,000 kilocalories of additional food energy each day. These include products such as Exceed® high-energy drink. This is one of the very few legitimate uses of a food supplement in sports. Taking in sufficient total food energy is essential in meeting the optimal nutritional needs of even the most sophisticated athlete.

In meeting the energy needs of the active young athlete, one should pay attention to the appropriate distribution of energy intake throughout the day. It is not uncommon to encounter athletes underperforming in afternoon practice sessions after having eaten no breakfast and only catch-as-catch-can lunch from the campus or high school corridor vending machine. These athletes' inability to perform between three and five o'clock in the afternoon should come as no surprise. The body has very limited ability to store its most readily available energy in the form of carbohydrates before it is converted to body fat. Body fat is a less efficient source of energy, as it must be mobilized from fat deposits and transferred to muscle cells before it can serve as an energy source for muscle work. Individuals who perform vigorous physical work during the day have always found regular food-energy intake spaced at intervals to be essential to good performance.

Eating the Right Foods

A varied diet sufficient in amount to satisfy energy needs will provide all of the essential nutrients the young athlete needs. Young athletes, their coaches, and particularly their parents are continually questioning the adequacy of the athlete's diet in providing all of those nutrients that are known to be essential for good health and athletic performance. Actually, there are approximately sixty substances recognized as so-called essential nutrients—substances that must be included in the daily diet. New dietary customs, fast foods, meatless diets, and skipped meals all raise questions as to whether the young woman or young man active in sports is adequately satisfying nutritional needs. Many coaches are asking, "Can you really 'do your thing' with a hamburger, fries, and a shake on Friday night, a pizza on Saturday, and another fast-food dinner another night during the week?" Thirty-five percent of a population of high school varsity basketball players ate their evening meal alone the night before they were interviewed in a recent nutrition study. As we've noted before, eating alone is likely to mean that you will not eat well.

Another factor that causes parents and coaches concern is the controversy surrounding special diets and dietary supplements. Some self-styled nutrition experts claim that without a particular "miracle" diet and/or supplement, we all run the risk of being chronically undernourished. Others promote the healing or empowering properties of certain herbs, remedies, or vitamins. It is difficult for the average adult—or adolescent—to sort out those claims. For the athlete, such nutritional solutions are, in fact, not only useless and expensive but perhaps dangerous. It is best to consult a physician or a legitimate nutrition scientist if there is real concern about nutritional needs.

Applying a simple diet evaluation scheme is the athlete's best protection against getting involved with useless, expensive, and dangerous supplements.

How the athlete insures the adequacy of his or her diet is important and can be the best protection against needless and expensive nutrient supplements. A simple and effective system of diet evaluation can be implemented by any parent or junior or senior high school athlete. Simply write down all of the food items eaten each day for three or four typical days. Then see if there are included in that diet appropriate representations of the four food groups that, most of us have learned, are essential to good diets. Each day, are there two servings of dairy foods, such as milk, cheese, ice cream, or yogurt? Are there two servings of high-protein foods, such as meats, fish, poultry, legumes, or beans? Are there four servings of fruits or vegetables? Are there four servings of grain foods, such as cereals, bread, or rolls? When these twelve servings are included in each day's diet, the athlete and parent can be confident that the intake of all the known essential nutrients is adequate to meet the needs of the most intensely training athlete. This diet makes any vitamin, mineral, protein, or other food supplement unnecessary.

Recently two high school athletes were seen in their physician's office on successive days with very similar complaints. Both were feeling unwell, with marked bone pain and severe pounding headaches that had kept them awake at night and prevented them from attending classes. This unusual combination of symptoms alerted the physician to ask whether the students had been taking any vitamin pills or supplements. Indeed they had been. Both were candidates for the football team in the upcoming autumn and were trying to "bulk up" to increase their weight and potential for making the team. They were each taking three cans daily of a liquid vitamin-and-protein mixture that was being sold by the coach. Laboratory tests demonstrated that they were both suffering from vitamin A poisoning, a serious, painful intoxication that takes many weeks to get over. Later we will outline safe and effective ways to increase playing weight for improved performance in certain sports. These do not include taking expensive and potentially dangerous protein-and-vitamin supplements unless prescribed by a physician.

For the active, healthy young athlete vitamin, protein, mineral, and amino acid supplements are useless, needlessly expensive, and potentially dangerous.

The athlete's diet that contains twelve servings with appropriate representation from the four food groups makes supplements unnecessary but won't meet the energy needs of the athlete. This basic four-food-group diet must be supplemented with second servings and preference foods to meet what may be very generous energy requirements.

- A good rule to follow is to eat first what you need (the twelve servings from the four food groups), then eat what you want to satisfy energy demands.

- A second rule is that if and when your diet is so inadequate that you need a vitamin or protein supplement, you don't need a supplement; you need a better diet. The athlete can never compete on a diet of pills and powders.

Meeting the Athlete's Need for Water and Salt

In addition to the athlete's unique need for increased intake of food energy to meet the demands of training and competing, another specific need of the athlete is replacement of the water lost in sweating. A large young athlete can lose ten or more pounds of water during an intense practice session. Basketball players in an air-conditioned gym were recently found to be losing four to six pounds of body water during a typical high school practice. Replacing these losses is critical both to continued good performance and avoidance of serious heat disorders, such as cramps, heat exhaustion, and heat stroke. Body water is involved in several functions critical to performance. The body's chemical processes that provide the energy for muscle work go on in water. All of the transport functions of oxygen, nutrients, and body wastes are carried on in body water. Of most importance to the exercising athlete is the fact that the large amount of heat generated by exercising muscles is transported by water in the blood to the skin, where water is essential for the production of sweat. Body heat is dissipated most efficiently through the evaporation of sweat on exposed skin surfaces. An abundant supply of body water, first to transport muscle-generated heat and then to produce the sweat needed for evaporative cooling, is the best insurance against the complications of heat cramps, heat exhaustion, and life-threatening heat stroke.

Water breaks are an important safety measure.

Losses of body water of as little as 2 percent of total body weight (three pounds for a 150-pound athlete, for example) will cause a very noticeable decrease in performance. With such water loss, energy production is compromised and endurance is limited. Preventing excessive body-water deficits by fluid intake prior to exercise and at intervals during exercise will contribute measurably to performance.

Early one September Monday morning, the telephone in the sports medicine clinic rang. On the line were a father, a mother, and a sixteen-year-old daughter, each on his or her own telephone extension. The daughter was a nationally ranked junior tennis champion who had just been defeated in the Midwest tennis championships played in St. Louis the preceding weekend. She had repeatedly defeated the person to whom she had lost the championship, but on this particular Sunday she faded badly as the match progressed.

This had been a most disappointing performance. In the opinion of her father, the tennis player had not eaten right, and he had decided that she should be "talked to" about her diet. Mother wondered if she should be taking more vitamins. Neither concern would appear to have caused her to blow a particular tennis match. You don't get to the Midwest championship finals if you are suffering from malnutrition.

We asked the daughter to run upstairs and weigh herself. She came back to report that some sixteen hours after her disastrous match, she weighed eight or nine pounds less than her normal pretournament weight. Playing in the heat of a St. Louis September weekend, she had not monitored her needs for water, had lost more than ten pounds of body water, had become dehydrated, and had underperformed. She admitted to a rather severe, throbbing headache and feeling faint for several hours after the match, an early symptom of impending heat exhaustion.

Biochemists and exercise scientists have studied the nature of sweat and have come up with some very interesting and important findings for the athlete. Sweat is a very dilute body fluid when compared to other body fluids. It contains less than one-third the concentration of salts that blood plasma contains, for example. It is interesting that the better conditioned the athlete, the more dilute and watery the sweat. When athletes sweat, they lose much more water than salt.

**Sweating results in an increase in the concentration
of the body's salts and minerals.**

Other interesting things that have been learned about sweat is that women have fewer sweat glands and produce less sweat than men. They have greater skin surface area for every pound of body weight, however, and unlike men, they dissipate more of the heat generated in exercise by convection and conduction from the skin than by evaporation. In contrast to what was thought some years ago, women tolerate exercise in the heat as well as men.

Prior to the onset of adolescence, children do not produce sweat efficiently. They have a limited capacity for evaporative heat loss from their bodies during exercise. However, it has been shown that they make a very early psychological adjustment to exertion in the heat, not noticing it as much as older individuals, even though their bodies' mechanisms for dissipating heat are poorly developed. This puts the young athlete at increased risk to heat exhaustion. Preventing heat disorders in very young athletes is an increasing concern as large numbers of preadolescent sport participants find themselves exercising in competitive situations in the heat of summer and early autumn. These very young athletes must have their practices and competitions modified or rescheduled during hot weather and have their fluid needs and the intensity of play carefully monitored. These most amateur of participants will be the last to know when they are at risk to heat exhaustion or even heat stroke. The preadolescent child is relatively new to the world of team competition and training.

**The increased risk of heat exhaustion of very young
athletes demands the attention of parents and
coaches.**

Water is the ideal beverage for replacing the fluid losses of the sweating athlete. The water should be refrigerator temperature, copious in amount, and provided in a hygienic container. So-called athlete drinks or sport drinks present several problems for the athlete losing body water through sweat. Sport drinks contain a variety of salts that, when added to the body, only increase the already elevated salt concentration of the dehydrated athlete. The concentration of salts and the masking sugar flavor cause these beverages to leave the stomach slowly, producing a sense of fullness and satiety. This actually discourages the athlete from taking in much-needed water. In addition, in the intense emotional environment of competition, all senses become heightened, making the distinctive flavor of certain beverages unpleasant and discouraging the intake of water.

With no such disadvantages, water remains a wonderfully inexpensive, ideal beverage for replacing the water losses of sweat. Every old sailor knows that you don't maintain hydration by drinking saltwater, but American merchandisers have sold salty water in pretty orange and green bottles to millions of athletes.

Athletes can very effectively monitor their needs for water replacement by recognizing that any weight that is lost in a period of a few hours or even a few days is essentially all water weight. With a pound of fat the equivalent of 3,500 kilocalories of energy, and the energy expenditure to run one mile approximately one hundred calories, it is apparent that any sudden changes in weight are not due to a significant change in the body's fat content. Nude weighing before and after each game or tournament match and drinking sufficient water to maintain a stable pretournament weight are highly desirable practices. During daily or twice-daily practices of any sport in warm, humid weather, it is recommended that all athletes record a nude weight before and after each practice. This is the surest way to be certain that fluid losses are replaced between practice sessions.

Tasting the salt in the perspiration running off the fevered brow during exercise obviously generates some real concern on the part of the athlete as to how these salt losses are to be replaced. Thus, many athletes are impressed with the much-promoted salt- and electrolyte-containing sport drinks. Fortunately, there has been some very elaborate research on this at outstanding exercise-physiology laboratories, such as Ball State University labs, and in the United States Department of Agriculture's Trace Metal Research Laboratory. These recent investigations document that *all of the salt and mineral losses of the most profusely sweating athlete are abundantly replaced by the elements in the generous mixed diet of the exercising athlete.* The kidneys sort out what of this dietary intake is needed for replacement of sweat losses and what can be excreted as waste into the urine. Taking extra minerals in drinks or salt tablets only taxes the body's normal mechanisms for maintaining a healthy mineral balance. Particularly threatening is the use of salt tablets, which athletes often take indiscriminately. A recent football heat-stroke victim was found to have fourteen salt tablets in his stomach on X-ray examination—salt that only accentuated the consequences of his severe dehydration.

Clean, cool water is the ideal beverage for athletes.

Young athletes should drink lots of clean, cool water. Eight to ten ounces drunk immediately before practice or a training run delays the adverse effects of copious sweat loss. In hot weather, coaches should schedule water breaks every twenty-five minutes and make generous amounts of water readily available to the athletes. Distance runners should drink water at each water stop during a race, and water intake should be scheduled by trainers or coaches during day-long meets, such as track events, gymnastic competitions, and wrestling tournaments. If the weather is warm and the competition particularly demanding, repeated nude weighing can give further assurance that the risks and handicaps of dehydration are being avoided.

Eating Before and During Competition

The annals of sports are replete with stories about pregame eating experiences that turned certain defeat into glorious victory. Soon after joining the sports medicine clinic at the University of Washington, one of us was asked by a young track star, "Say, Doc, why is pizza such a fast food?" The response he got—complete ignorance of why pizza is a "fast" food, or even that it had ever been known to make people run fast—cost medical science some credibility in the eyes of this speedy quarter-miler. In the not-too-distant past, some local runner had enjoyed a large intake of pizza and ran the best race of his career. Others merely put two and two together, and to the satisfaction of the pizza-parlor operator and a few subsequent generations of runners at this school, pizza became a fast food. The pizza was traditionally eaten at one particular establishment (not the best in the area) on Fridays before every Saturday track meet and was actually eaten by all of the believers in complete silence!

**The psychological impact of the pregame meal
should not be minimized or ignored.**

The pregame meal can serve the needs of the athlete and the team to exploit the very real emotional impact of food and eating together. In planning the pregame meal, you should keep in mind the most important thing: that it should be planned. A well-planned eating experience tells athletes that they are being well prepared to handle their responsibilities in the upcoming competition.

Here are guidelines for planning the pregame meal for an athlete or a team:

- Locate a suitable place where the team or athletes can be together and can concentrate on the upcoming competition.

- Include in the menu any food that the athletes "know" will make them win.

- The meal is best if it is low in fat, modest in protein, and high in carbohydrate.

- The meal should be modest in amount.

- The menu should avoid those foods that carry a greater-than-usual risk of food poisoning, such as cream gravies, turkey, and cream pastries.

- Fatty foods leave the stomach slowly and thus should be eaten five or more hours before a competitive event.

Having had nothing to eat for several hours, many athletes will play "hungry." Coaches and athletes should all learn the old rule, *Saturday's game is played on Wednesday, Thursday, and Friday's food intake.* The pregame meal is not the time to try to provide all of the energy for some high-energy-expending competition.

A big steak dinner is a poor choice as a pregame meal.

A very simple pregame menu that can be arranged in any commercial eating establishment, is not expensive, and can be eaten two and a half to three hours before the game includes the following:

- Lean beef or chicken sandwiches

- Pitchers of fruit punch or fruit juice

- A large Jell-O salad

- Generous servings of sherbet and cake or cookies

As young athletes become increasingly serious about their sport commitments, there are those who direct their precompetition anxieties to their stomachs and upper gastrointestinal tracts. They may experience precompetition diarrhea or be pregame vomiters. These delightfully intense individuals can profit by being introduced to complete liquid pregame meals. Products such as Exceed® come in small cans, which can be chilled and sipped up to an hour or two before game time. Certain athletes find these products the answer to food intake during day-long competition, such as track meets, gymnastics competitions, and wrestling tournaments.

Special attention should be given to the food needs of the team of young athletes away from home, those who are spending an evening in a motel between episodes of competition. These young people are at considerable risk for gastronomical disasters and compromised performance the following day. It is as important to plan evening eating as it is to plan all mealtime food intake. Sherbet and cookies make a good high-carbohydrate evening snack. By providing such refreshments, the coach or manager may keep the athletes away from vending machines and fast-food establishments and make a positive contribution to the energy taken into the next day's game.

Special Nutritional Needs of the High School Athlete

As young men and women begin to make their serious commitment to sports during their high school years, they encounter nutrition and training procedures designed specifically to optimize their potential for performance in a given sport. At the high school level, the most common procedures are cutting weight for participation in strength or weight-matched sports, building up (increasing body weight), and loading up on glycogen for endurance sports. All these practices can be safe when properly carried out and can contribute to the participant's success and enjoyment in the sport. The team physician, family physician, or professional nutritionist may be called upon to initiate these special nutrition practices in the young, growing athlete.

Weight Control in Sports

Many late-maturing small individuals are attracted to interscholastic wrestling because the competitors in this sport are matched on a weight basis and the small size of the individual is not a handicap. In addition to small late maturers in the lower weight classes, many young men weighing 120 to 150 pounds who are too small to be competitive in football or basketball find wrestling an attractive winter sport. In fact, there is a disproportionate number of participants in the weight classes between 120 and 145 pounds, so competition for varsity positions at these weight classes may be very intense. The wrestlers often try to manipulate their weights to compete in a weight class in which they think they may have the best chance of being on the first team. This can lead to serious abuses, such as fluid restriction, starvation, and use of diuretic pills and cathartics.

> **The goal for most effective participation in a weight-matched sport is to take into competition the maximum amount of strength, endurance, and quickness for every pound of body weight.**

The athlete should go into competition with a minimal level of fatness compatible with optimal fitness. The estimated minimal-fatness level of 5 to 7 percent of body weight satisfies this goal and has been found to be the level of fatness of high-performing

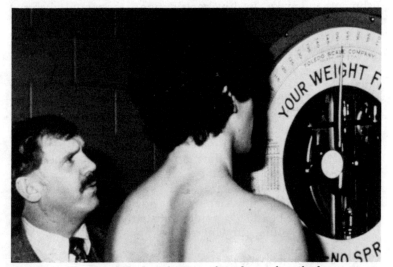

Weight control should be based upon safe and sound methods.

wrestlers and other elite athletes in weight-matched sports. It is recommended that every candidate for the wrestling team have his body fat estimated six to eight weeks before the competing season begins. When the athlete knows what his fatness level is, he can calculate what his competing weight would be at 5 to 7 percent body fat. He then knows that he can be most competitive at that weight, allowing three to four pounds for growth during the season. Most candidates have excess fat that must be lost to reach their desired competing weights. This can be done by increasing their energy expenditures with after-school, preseason conditioning and by limiting their diets to no less than 2,000 calories each day. The rate of fatness loss should be no greater than two or three pounds per week. Thus it is essential to initiate the program well before the competing season. *There is no way in which fat can be reduced rapidly without sacrificing normal growth and reducing muscle.*

In certain strength-related sports, such as men's gymnastics and figure skating, fat in excess of the minimum compatible with optimal fitness will hinder performance. As in wrestling, estimating fatness and reducing it with modest diet reductions and increased energy expenditure at a carefully controlled rate will be compatible with good performance and good health.

"Bulking Up" for Sport

Each year hundreds of thousands of young adolescents try to increase their body weight and size to increase their potential for sport performance. In a study of forty-eight varsity football players in four different high schools, more than two-thirds of them had used special diets, drugs, and supplements to try to increase body weight at some time during their high school careers. The young person trying to increase body size for a sport needs professional supervision by a physician who appreciates the sincere commitment of the athlete and the importance of his or her concern with body size.

An interested physician can play a critical role in a young person's weight-gaining efforts by estimating maturity status and growth potential and recommending safe and effective methods for gain in muscle weight. The athlete must realize that only an increase in muscle mass will increase his or her potential as an athlete. Simply getting fatter will accomplish nothing and may threaten later health.

Only muscle work will increase muscle size and muscle mass. There is no hormone, vitamin, protein, or nutritional supplement that will increase muscle tissue.

The athlete trying to gain weight must follow a professionally supervised weight-training program of muscle work and must ingest the increased amount of food needed to support the increased growth of new muscle. This diet should be one low in cholesterol and saturated fats, limited in salt, and high in fiber content. (The American Heart Association has excellent instructions for diets of this type.) A diet for weight-gaining purposes in high school can be a very positive nutrition-education experience for young athletes and their families. In our experience, a conscientious high school athlete can gain as much as one to one and one-half pounds a week with a well-supervised program and a high degree of enthusiastic compliance.

Glycogen Loading for the Endurance Athlete

Relatively few young athletes at the junior or senior high school level become involved in competitions that are positively influenced by so-called glycogen loading, or supercompensation. Long-distance cross-country skiing and marathon running are classic examples of sports in which maximizing the concentration of muscle starch—glycogen—enhances the athlete's performance. Muscle glycogen concentrations are maximized by vigorously exercising the muscles used in the sport event for three or four days while maintaining a controlled amount of carbohydrate in the diet. The resulting depletion of glycogen in the muscle stimulates muscle enzymes to overcompensate the level of glycogen that is retained in the muscle when the athlete then takes in a high-carbohydrate diet. While ingesting the high-carbohydrate diet, the athlete must reduce the intensity of the training for four days prior to the competition. Glycogen loading is a very demanding regime and appropriate only for seriously committed athletes in true endurance events.

CHAPTER 6

CHAPTER 6
SPORT INJURIES:
When the Colors of Sports Are Black and Blue

Fortunately, serious injuries are not common in sports. This is particularly true for athletes less than fourteen years of age. Their small size and limited strength and aggressiveness, combined with safety rules and adult supervision, help minimizes the risk of significant injury. Sport injuries become more common in high school, where the intensity of competition increases along with the size and strength of the participants. These older and stronger athletes are more capable of causing injury to themselves and to their opponents.

Happily, regardless of age, most athletes will not suffer serious sport injuries, and when properly managed, injuries will limit training and competition for no more than a few days. Because responsibility for the recognition and management of sport-related injuries often falls on parents, there is some essential information that you should have about their nature and treatment.

What Is a Sport Injury?

The sore muscles Dad suffered the morning after a three-hour volleyball game at last summer's office picnic is not technically a sport injury. Those hurts are merely Nature's way of telling Dad that he should probably do some regular physical exercise. There are certain symptoms, however, that indicate a true sport injury and should be recognized as such by the athlete, the coach, and the parent. These include:

- Bleeding

- Mental confusion or loss of consciousness

- Numbness or tingling of an extremity

- A recognizable deformity of any body part
- Instability of any joint, such as a knee that "wobbles"
- The sound of tearing or ripping at the time of injury
- Localized swelling or pain
- Absence of a full range of motion of any joint

An individual with any of these symptoms should not return to play or practice until a very specific diagnosis of the nature of the injury has been made and the symptoms of injury have completely disappeared. Any of these injuries can easily be made worse by continued participation. Unable to move normally and protect themselves when injured, athletes with any of these symptoms are at high risk to a new injury.

The most common sport-related injuries are the so-called overuse injuries, the too-much, too-soon, too-fast injuries.

Overuse injuries result from the improper or excessive use of some body part, most often tendons and muscles. Overuse injuries are often identified with certain sports or types of activities. There is the jogger's heel, the jumper's knee, the tennis elbow, the swimmer's shoulder, the Little League elbow, and so on. All are the result of overuse of a specific muscle or tendon unit in training for a certain sport.

In collision sports, such as football, wrestling, ice hockey, and lacrosse, the most common injuries are bumps, bruises, and lacerations. In both collision and running sports, muscles, tendons, and ligaments can be stretched or torn in strains and sprains, although most of these possible injuries tend to be minor ones.

The injured athlete or the parents of the youth sport participant must assume primary responsibility for the proper management of a sport injury, initiating and following a safe and effective management plan that will assure the athlete's return to participation as quickly and as safely as possible. Prompt treatment and effective follow-through on a sound treatment plan are most important. Postponing care or failing to follow the prescribed treatment plan will prolong discomfort, hamper performance, and greatly increase the risk of reinjury.

Athletes should be told to inform their coach or trainer about any injury immediately so that they can be promptly treated and returned to the game or practice as soon as possible. Attempting to tough it out and play through pain can harm both the athlete and the team. It is better to stay out of practice for two or three days while an injury is being properly treated and return to action only when fully recovered.

Things *Not* to Do If Injured in Sport

Here are some important don'ts to emphasize to your young athlete:

- *Don't* try to hide an injury. Report the injury to the coach or trainer.

- *Don't* apply treatment other than simple first aid until a specific diagnosis has been made by the trainer or a doctor.

- *Don't* apply heat to an injury without orders from the doctor. A widely held but mistaken belief is that heat helps a new injury. As we'll see, it can actually make things worse rather than better.

- *Don't* use an injured part if it hurts. More pain means more injury.

- *Don't* take any drugs unless they are prescribed by a physician.

- *Don't* tape or splint an injured part without specific instructions from a doctor.

- *Don't* go back to practice or competition until you have a full range of motion, full strength (both sides are equally strong), and full function of the injured part.

These don'ts should be modified only under the direct orders of a physician or a certified trainer (not a volunteer or student trainer). The quickest and safest way to get back into active participation is to limit activity as long as there is any pain or swelling, then to follow rigidly the prescribed rehabilitation program, which will include a schedule of specifically planned exercises. In specialized sports medicine clinics, the patient problem most frequently seen is the athlete with an inadequately rehabilitated sport injury who returned to his sport and was reinjured. In a recent large study of high school football injuries, 50 percent of those injured were reinjured when they returned to participation—a sad commentary on injury management.

Things to Do When Injured

The athlete's first responsibility when injured is to get out of the game or practice. Continued participation may make the injury worse and may place the athlete at increased risk to another injury. A healthy substitute is better for the team than an injured all-star.

When leaving the field or court, the athlete should avoid using the injured part. The player should support an injured arm or wrist (with a sling if possible) and get support so he or she won't walk on an injured leg or ankle.

Never apply heat to a sport injury unless it is ordered by a physician.

Promptly apply the only first-aid treatment that is safe for treatment of a sport injury without professional advice—ICE (I for ice, C for compression, and E for elevation). The ICE treatment is

ICE—Ice, Compression, and Elevation—are safe and effective methods for dealing with injuries.

easily applied and easily available on the sidelines at games and practices. All that is needed are plastic bags (from the supermarket produce counter), crushed ice (from a nearby drive-in or school cafeteria), and a picnic cooler, which holds the bags of crushed ice and some wet four-inch elastic bandages.

To apply the ICE treatment, remove any part of the uniform that surrounds the injured area and elevate the arm or leg above the level of the heart. Apply one layer of the cold, wet elastic bandage on the skin directly over the injury, put the plastic bag of ice on the bandage, and firmly wrap the remainder of the bandage around the bag of ice. Keep the ice and the compression wrap on the elevated, immobilized injury for twenty-five to thirty minutes. As long as there is pain and/or swelling, keep the injury elevated. Avoid standing or walking on a painful leg or ankle before or after the ice application. ICE treatment for twenty-five to thirty minutes may be applied four or more times a day for a few days following an injury. If pain or swelling persists, see a physician.

When a girl sprains her ankle in a basketball game and its supporting ligaments are stretched and torn, or when a wide receiver strains and ruptures the fibers of a hamstring muscle, a sequence of events occurs that is common to all such sport injuries: Blood vessels are damaged and some will break, allowing blood and fluid to accumulate in the injured area. This causes increased pressure, swelling, and pain, and the pressure and swelling cause further damage and injury to the surrounding tissues.

This reaction of the body to injury has a protective function as well. The pain of the initial injury causes the muscles of the injured area to go into further painful spasms. This limits movement and discourages the use of the injured area, thereby preventing further injury.

The ICE treatment helps in three important ways:

- First, applying ice chills the bruised or injured area, causing blood vessels to contract and reducing circulation to the injured area—quite the opposite of what heat applications might do.

- Second, applying pressure with the elastic bandage inhibits the accumulation of blood and fluids in the area, thereby minimizing painful and damaging swelling.

- Finally, elevating the injury decreases fluid accumulation in the injured area, puts the area at rest, and helps reduce painful muscle spasms.

When applied promptly and repeatedly, ICE treatments significantly reduce the discomfort and period of limited activity resulting from an injury. Almost anything else—including heat applications—can cause harm in some instances.

When properly applied, ICE treatments can do no harm to any type of injury.

The story of Mark, a guard on a basketball team for thirteen-and fourteen-year-olds, is a case in point. He was playing in a city-wide postseason tournament when in the middle of the third quarter, he broke free for a lay-up. As he came down from the basket, his foot came down on the foot of the trailing opponent. He fell heavily, with his weight on the outer edge of his foot. It collapsed under him, painfully stretching and tearing portions of the ligaments on the outside of his left ankle.

The physician in attendance at the tournament examined the ankle, diagnosed a moderately severe sprain, and determined that an X-ray examination wasn't needed at the time. A volunteer trainer properly equipped with plastic ice bags and chilled, wet elastic bandages applied ice and compression to the injured ankle and had Mark elevate the ankle on an upper bleacher during the remainder of the game.

At the end of the game, supported by his teammates, Mark showered and was driven home, where thirty-minute ICE treatments were applied three more times before bedtime. A suitcase was used to elevate the foot of Mark's bed while he slept. (A pillow under the ankle is not recommended; it only stays in place for about the first three minutes of sleep.)

Mark remained at home watching the NCAA basketball championships with his father during the weekend. He used crutches rented from a local pharmacy for essential movements and applied the ICE treatment every three hours for thirty minutes. On Monday he used the crutches to go to school, applied the ICE treatment in the nurse's office during his two free periods, and checked in with his physician after school. By now there remained only slight swelling and some discoloration around the injured ankle. Mark could walk without pain. He was not allowed "essential walking" without crutches and began a series of progressive muscle-strengthening exercises.

The spring soccer season was to start in three weeks, and thus Mark was conscientious about his rehabilitation program. By doing the ankle-strengthening exercises three times each day, he was able to begin jogging in a week, to do full running in two weeks, and to cut and do sharp turns in three weeks. Mark was able to work out with his soccer team in time. He had also learned how to wrap his ankle and was advised to do so when exercising for the next year.

Although it took nearly a month, this was an excellent recovery from a moderately severe ankle sprain—a very common injury. The rapid and complete recovery was the result of repeated use of the ICE treatment, support and crutches to avoid further injury to the area, and the program of rehabilitation exercises. Mark's future participation in sports will not be limited by the persistent weak ankle that so many athletes complain of.

Preventing Sport Injuries

Everyone involved in youth sports should constantly seek practical ways to minimize the risk of sport injury. Here are some things parents, program directors, and athletes can do to reduce the risk of injury:

- Assure that competition is between persons with similar levels of proficiency, maturity, size, and strength. This is particularly important in the collision sports, where the risk of injury is greatest. The less-skilled and smaller players get more than their share of injuries in such sports.

- Be sure that athletes are at appropriate levels of conditioning before they turn out for practice or attempt vigorous competition. A good idea for athletes is to talk to the coach two or three months prior to the first workouts and get suggestions for a preseason conditioning program. The unconditioned athlete gets injured early in the season, sometimes seriously.

- Be certain that protective equipment is available and used. Protective equipment has been developed and provided for good reasons. Be sure it fits, that it doesn't need repair, and that it is used properly.

- Most sports are played on the feet. Be certain that shoes and socks fit and that socks are clean and without holes. Many troublesome foot problems can be prevented.

- Don't wear jewelry in active sports. Neck jewelry can be dangerous; rings can produce serious finger injury by getting caught in basket nets, uniforms, and so on.

- Practice good hygiene. Skin infections are common among athletes and can keep an athlete out of training for a week or more of expensive treatment. They can also spread to other team members. Showering with an antibacterial soap daily is a good practice to reduce the risk of skin infections. Keep all uniforms laundered and clean.

- Fingernails should always be trimmed shorter than the tip of the finger to prevent painful scratches and potentially serious eye injuries. This is especially important in basketball.

- Never play with a fever. Otherwise mild, common viral infections can become serious illnesses following a hard workout or game. Stay home; the risk of passing an infection on to other team members should always be avoided. A good rule is that with fever over 100 degrees, stay home and get well.

- Whether at a school, playground, or community gymnasium, take a minute to be sure that anything a player may run into or get injured from is well away from the playing area. Bicycles, automobiles, benches, lawn mowers, sprinklers, scorers' tables, and other obstacles can all cause serious injuries.

Be Prepared for an Emergency

Most injuries occurring in sports are minor, but on very rare occasions, serious, life-threatening injuries occur. These emergencies usually have to be managed on the scene before any medical help is available. In professionally supervised school sports, at practice and during games, the coach or trainer will be responsible for a plan of action to be followed in an emergency. In the community sport programs in which most children participate or at unsupervised pickup games, there will be no professionally trained coach or trainer on hand.

In these situations we strongly recommend that volunteer coaches, parents, and athletes over the age of twelve do one thing before getting involved any further in sports: Get certified in CPR (cardiopulmonary resuscitation). CPR training is available through the American Red Cross, local fire departments, schools, or Boy Scout programs.

Training in CPR teaches the simple life-saving techniques that can keep a seriously injured athlete alive until emergency medical help arrives.

An accident or injury to an athlete that results in any of the following symptoms presents a serious emergency that demands the skills of CPR training and prompt medical assistance:

- Not breathing
- Unconscious
- Bleeding
- In shock—particularly during hot weather

Injured athletes in these conditions can die before medical assistance arrives on the scene if someone isn't prepared to initiate thoughtful action.

Before you as a parent attend your daughter's or son's next game or practice, or before you as a young athlete start that pickup game with your friends, take ten seconds and think through exactly how you would get emergency help if one of those very rare but life-threatening injuries should occur.

You must know the answers to the following questions:

- Where is there a telephone?
- Who has the coins to make it work?
- Whom do you call for help?
- What is the location of the field or gym?
- Will the emergency vehicle be able to get on the field? If there is a locked gate, who has the key?

If you don't know these things, you may be helpless when the crisis occurs. Someone's son or daughter or teammate could die because no one was prepared for the unexpected.

Earlier we listed some important don'ts for sport injuries in general. The following recommendations are even more critical because of the life-threatening nature of some serious injuries:

- *Don't* move an unconscious player any more than needed for CPR.

- *Don't* move any player who can't move all four extremities freely.

- *Don't* remove the helmet from an unconscious player. You may seriously compound a possible injury to the spine.

- *Don't* use ammonia capsules to attempt to revive the player who may be unconscious or "dinged." They can complicate a neck or spine injury and may cause face and eye burns.

Steve and his friends were to be the stalwarts of this year's local Babe Ruth baseball team. They decided to get together for an informal Saturday afternoon game the week before practice was to begin. Shortly after the game started, Steve raced for second base and slid headfirst toward the bag. As he slid, his left arm caught on the base and his legs became tan-

Severe injuries demand immediate medical attention.

gled with the feet of the second baseman, who was covering the bag. Steve's back bent in a severe arch. He heard a crack and felt an excruciating pain. As his teammates gathered around, he cried out that he couldn't move his legs. Brad, the catcher, took charge and ordered that no one move or even touch Steve. Brad ran to the bench, opened his gear bag, and took out a card and a twenty-five-cent piece he had taped inside. He ran to the telephone booth at the parking lot. Depositing the quarter, he dialed 911 and reported the following: "There has been an injury at the baseball diamond in Seahurst Park at Fifteenth and Collins streets. A player has hurt his back and can't move his legs."

In less than five minutes, medics were on the field. Steve was moved by expert medical-aid personnel and within minutes was in the hospital and being taken care of by specialists. Steve had broken a bone in his back, but his legs were not permanently paralyzed. He actually played the last four games of the season.

Lots of people say that Steve was very lucky. But Brad, Steve, Steve's parents, and his doctors know that luck had little to do with it. Someone—Brad—knew what to do and was prepared to do it. Steve was lucky all right—lucky that Brad was there, for the specialist told Steve's parents that he could easily have been paralyzed if he had been moved incorrectly.

Never encourage an athlete to play with pain.

Much of the fun and satisfaction of sport participation comes from extending oneself to maximum effort. Such stresses may on occasion result in injury. Although most injuries are not serious, they do interfere temporarily with one's ability to compete and can result in more serious injuries if not cared for properly. Know how to manage the more common, less severe injuries that will be brought home by young athletes. Don't let them become more severe than need be or lead to a needlessly prolonged period of disability.

CHAPTER 7

CHAPTER 7
ATHLETIC STRESS:
Developing Coping Skills
Through Sports

Sport participation places both physical and psychological demands on athletes. From youth leagues to the professional level, athletes are forced to cope with the stresses that arise from competing head-on with others in activities that are important to the athletes and to others, such as parents, coaches, and peers. Some athletes learn to cope successfully with these stresses, and for them sports are enjoyable and challenging. Others who are unable to cope find sport participation to be a stressful and threatening experience.

There is no question that people differ in their ability to cope successfully with stressful situations. Such differences result primarily from the attitudes and coping skills that are learned during the childhood and adolescent years. Athletics can be an important arena in which such skills are learned. In a sense, the athletic experience can be a sort of laboratory for trying out and mastering ways of dealing with stress.

Through their athletic experiences, youngsters can develop attitudes, beliefs, and coping skills that carry over into other areas of their lives. Childhood is the best time to learn stress-management skills, and in this chapter we are concerned with what you as a parent can do to help in this process.

What Is Stress?

Before discussing ways of reducing stress, we need to explore what we mean by stress. An examination of what stress is should give us some clues on how to cope successfully with it.

We typically use the term *stress* in two different but related ways. First, we use the term to refer to *situations* in our lives that place physical or psychological demands on us. Family conflicts, work pressures, or school problems are examples of events that might cause us to say that "there is a lot of stress in my life right now."

The second way in which we use the term is to refer to our mental, emotional, and behavioral *responses* to these demanding situations. Worry, anger, tension, or depression are examples of such reactions, as are loss of appetite, sleep difficulties, and inability to get one's mind off the problem. We are referring to such reactions when we say, "I'm feeling a lot of stress right now."

In the accompanying figure, we present an analysis of stress that takes both the situation and the person's reactions into account. As you can see, four major elements are involved.

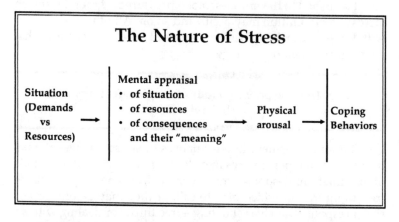

The Nature of Stress

Situation (Demands vs Resources) → Mental appraisal
• of situation
• of resources
• of consequences and their "meaning" → Physical arousal → Coping Behaviors

The first element is the external situation that is making some sort of physical or psychological demand on the person. Typically we view our emotions as being directly triggered by these "pressure" situations, as shown in such statements as "He makes me furious when he says that" or "The kids drove me nuts today." This, however, is not the case. The true emotional triggers are not in the external situation; they are in our minds. Situations in and of themselves have no meaning to us until we *appraise* them, which is the second element of stress. Through the process of appraisal, we perceive and give meaning to situations. This evaluation process has several parts.

- First of all, we appraise the nature of the situation and the demands it is placing upon us.

- At the same time we appraise the resources that we have to deal with it. We judge, in other words, how capable we are of coping with the situation.

- We also judge the probable consequences of coping or failing to cope with the situation and the meaning of those consequences for us.

The emotional responses that we call stress are likely to occur when we view ourselves as incapable of coping with a high-demand situation that has potentially harmful consequences for us. In response to such appraisals, our body instantaneously mobilizes itself to deal with the emergency, and we experience physiological arousal, the third element of stress. This inborn fight-or-flight response involves a general arousal of the body. Heart rate increases, blood is rushed to the muscles, blood pressure and muscle tension increase, perspiration may occur, and so on. All of us are familiar with the way our body becomes aroused when we perceive that we are threatened or in danger.

The stress response includes thoughts, feelings, and behaviors.

The fourth element in our analysis of stress involves the behaviors that the person uses in order to try to cope with demands of the situation. Responses may be mental, as when a quarterback tries to figure out which play to call, or they may be physical or social responses, such as shooting a free throw or dealing with an angry opponent.

To view this sequence in action, let us consider Kevin, who is at the plate with two outs, the bases loaded, and his team trailing by a run in the last inning. He is facing a pitcher who has struck him out twice without his even hitting a foul ball. He views the pitcher as being too tough for him (demands exceed resources). He thinks that if he strikes out again, his parents, coach, and teammates will be disappointed in him and he will be disappointed in himself. These appraisals of the situation, his ability to cope with it, and the negative consequences he expects combine to produce predictable physical results. His mouth is as dry as a ball of cotton. His legs are shaking and he can barely hold the bat. His stomach is churning and his heart is pounding. His responses to the situation involve trying to concentrate on the pitcher and swing only at balls that are in the strike zone. Whatever the outcome of his actions, it is clear that Kevin is experiencing a high degree of stress.

Kevin's stress response to the situation seems quite natural. Most of us would probably react in much the same way. Yet some would argue that situations such as this place too much stress on children before they are psychologically equipped to handle it. Are youth sports indeed too stressful for children?

How Stressful Are Youth Sports?

Researchers have used various approaches to try to measure the stressfulness of the youth sport setting. In several studies electronic devices were attached to children so that their physiological arousal could be measured directly, through a method known as telemetry. The instruments send a radio signal to a receiver so that physiological responses, such as heart rate, can be measured while the subject is behaving normally. These studies have shown that children can experience high levels of arousal during athletic contests. For example, heart rates averaging nearly 170 beats per minute have been recorded in male Little League Baseball players while they were at bat.

The problem with this approach, however, is that physiological measures by themselves cannot tell us exactly *which* emotion is being experienced by the child. In some children elevated heart rates may reflect high levels of anxiety, while in others they may reflect simple excitement or elation. We can't tell merely by measuring the level of arousal.

To get around this problem, another approach has been to ask children to fill out rating scales of how tense, anxious, or worried they are at a particular moment. In a series of studies conducted at UCLA, Tara Scanlan and Michael Passer obtained anxiety ratings from boys and girls immediately before and after youth soccer matches. They found that most children reported rather low levels of anxiety at both points in time. However, about 20 percent of the children reported high levels of stress before the game, and many of the children reported high anxiety after games that their teams had lost.

There is evidence that sports can be stressful, at least for some children.

How stressful are sports compared with other activities in which children participate? To answer this important question, Julie Simon and Rainer Martens of the University of Illinois obtained anxiety ratings from nine- to fourteen-year-old boys before a number of different activities, including various individual and team sports, school tests, and band solos. The researchers found that none of the sports they studied aroused as much anxiety as band solos. Moreover, wrestling was the only sport that was more anxiety-arousing than classroom tests in school. Of the various sports studied, individual sports caused the highest levels of pre-event anxiety. But, like the UCLA researchers, Simon and Martens reported that some of the young athletes experienced extremely high levels of stress before competing, regardless of the sport.

Taken together, the research results suggest that sport partici-pation is not exceedingly stressful for most children, especially in comparison with other activities in which children have their per-formance evaluated. But it is equally clear that the sport setting is capable of producing high levels of stress for certain children. In-stead of finding athletic competition enjoyable and challenging, some children undoubtedly experience threats and anxiety in the competitive sport setting. Such youngsters could surely benefit from attempts to help them cope more effectively with the stress that threatens their enjoyment of the sport activity.

How Stress Affects Young Athletes

Fear and anxiety are unpleasant emotions that most people try to avoid. There is evidence that this is precisely what many stress-ridden young athletes do. Avoiding or dropping out of sports is one of the ways some children escape from an activity they find threatening rather than pleasant. Canadian researchers Terry Orlick and Cal Botterill held extensive interviews with children who were not participating in sports. Many of them had quit sport programs. A large proportion of these youngsters indicated that they would like to compete but were fearful of performing poorly or of failing to make a team. Stress can thus reduce enjoyment and participation in athletics.

In recent years, the notion of burnout has received increasing attention in sports. Elite athletes and coaches have dropped out of sports at the peak of their careers, maintaining that they are too "burned-out" to continue. Likewise, youth sport authorities have become increasingly concerned about the large numbers of youth who are dropping out of sports during the adolescent years. While research suggests that in many cases, children drop out because they become more interested in other things, there is also concern that intense competitive pressures and too many sport demands may cause some youngsters to burn out and abandon sports. Sport burnout is a legitimate concern, since burned out athletes often show depression, loss of drive and energy, and a lowered sense of self-esteem that carries over into other areas of their lives.

Stress affects not only how athletes feel but also how they perform. All of us have seen athletes fall apart or "choke" under high levels of stress. When under great stress, even gifted athletes can perform poorly. A key to understanding how stress affects performance is the relationship between physical arousal and performance shown in the accompanying figure.

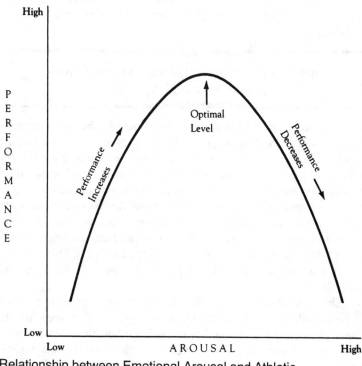

Relationship between Emotional Arousal and Athletic Performance

This relationship takes the form of an upside-down U. When arousal is absent or extremely low, athletes frequently describe themselves as flat and do not perform as well as they are able. As arousal increases, so does performance, but only up to a certain point. Beyond that optimal arousal point at the top of the inverted U, arousal begins to interfere with behavior, and we get a drop-off in performance. Research has also shown that the more complicated or difficult the task, the less arousal it takes to interfere with performance. Thus, it takes less arousal to interfere with a figure skater's or a golfer's performance than with a sprinter's or a weight lifter's.

High-stress athletes who cannot control their emotions are likely to experience higher-than-optimal levels of arousal and to perform poorly. The failure experiences that result only serve to reinforce these athletes' fears and undermine their confidence. Thus, a vicious circle involving anxiety, impaired performance, and increased anxiety can result. Many young athletes never succeed in achieving their potential in sports because of their inability to control their anxiety.

There is an optimal level of arousal beyond which performance begins to suffer.

One other effect of stress should be noted. There is mounting medical evidence that high levels of chronic stress can impair health. The physical nature of the stress response taxes the resources of the body and appears to make children and adults alike more susceptible to illness and disease. Sports medicine specialists have observed many cases of health breakdowns of various sorts among highly stressed children. Not long ago, we saw a twelve-year-old competitive figure skater who was experiencing so much stress related to her sport that she developed an ulcer. This is surely a high and unnecessary price to pay for the pursuit of athletic excellence!

Stress affects physical well-being in yet another way: Studies of both college and high school athletes show that stressful life changes are related to an increased likelihood of injury. Sports medicine specialists have also observed that athletes who find participation to be stressful and unpleasant often appear to take longer to recover from injuries. It may be that in some cases, an athlete finds in an injury a temporary and legitimate haven from the stresses of competition.

We see, then, that stress can have many effects on athletes of all ages and that most of them are negative. Thus, athletes who develop coping skills that allow them to bear up under the pressure of competition, to be mentally tough in the face of athletic challenge and adversity, have a definite advantage.

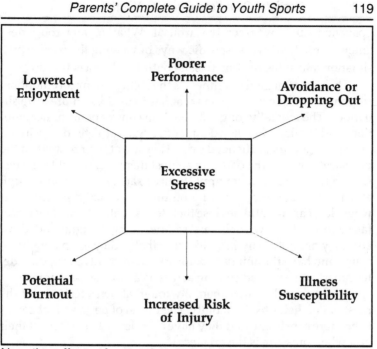

Negative effects of excessive stress in youth sports

The Nature of Mental Toughness

One of the highest compliments that can be paid to an athlete is to be labeled "mentally tough." Some coaches and athletes speak of mental toughness as if it were a quality that a person either has or does not have. In reality, however, mental toughness is not something we are born with; rather, it is a set of specific, learned attitudes and skills.

The specific skills that constitute what we call mental toughness fall within the brackets of the stress model described above. Mentally tough athletes mentally appraise themselves and pressure situations in ways that arouse a positive desire to achieve rather than a fear of failure. Freedom from the disruptive effects of fear of failure allows them to concentrate on the task instead of worrying about the terrible things that will happen if they fail in the situation. Another specific skill that contributes to mental toughness is the ability to keep physical arousal within manageable limits. Somehow, these athletes are able to "psych up" with enough arousal to optimize their performance without being "psyched out" by excessive arousal. What mental toughness amounts to, therefore, is specific ways of viewing the competitive situation and skills relating to self-control and concentration.

The core of mental toughness is the ability to control emotional responses and concentrate on what has to be done in pressure situations. The mentally tough athlete is in control of his or her emotions and is calm and relaxed under fire. Such athletes do not avoid pressure; they are challenged by it. They are at their best when the pressure is on and the odds are against them. Being put to the test is not a threat but another opportunity to achieve. Mentally tough athletes are able to concentrate on the task at hand in situations where less capable athletes lose their focus of attention. They rarely fall victim to their own or others' self-defeating thoughts and ideas, and they are not easily intimidated. Finally, they are mentally resilient and have the ability to bounce back from adversity, their determination to succeed coming across as a quiet self-assurance.

It is no accident that mentally tough athletes tend to get the most out of their physical ability. Their level of performance seems to be more consistent, and they have a tendency to perform at their best when pressure is the greatest.

Mental toughness is a set of specific, learnable skills which can give a youngster the winning edge not only in sports, but in life.

As a parent, you are in a position to help your young athlete develop the skills that comprise mental toughness. In doing so, you can help sports to serve as a catalyst in their personal development.

Reducing Stress and Building Mental Toughness

Fear of Failure: The Athlete's Worst Enemy

Aside from fears of physical injury that produce stress for some athletes, most athletic stress arises from the fact that sports are an important social situation. The athlete's performance is visible to everyone present, and it is constantly being evaluated by the athlete and by significant people in his or her life. Many athletes dread the possibility of failure and fear the disapproval of others. Some feel that their athletic performance is a reflection of their basic self-worth, and they therefore have a great need to avoid failing. They are convinced that failure will diminish them in their own eyes and in the eyes of others.

We are convinced that fear of failure is the athlete's worst enemy. The thinking of high-stress athletes is dominated by negative thoughts and worries about failing. Unchecked, these concerns with failure undermine confidence, enthusiasm, the willingness to invest and persist, and, most importantly, the athlete's belief in himself or herself. It is these thoughts that transform the competitive athletic situation from what should be a welcome challenge to a threatening and unpleasant pressure-cooker. It is these thoughts that trigger the high physical arousal that interferes with performance and with the ability to concentrate fully on the task at hand.

Fear of failure underlies most instances of "choking" under pressure.

The ideas that underlie fear of failure do not arise in a vacuum. They almost always have been communicated to youngsters by their parents or by other important adults. This is not surprising, because the basic beliefs underlying such ideas are very widespread and accepted in our culture, which emphasizes achievement as a measure of personal worth. In our society, an untold number of children fall victim to their parents' demands that they perform exactly as expected, and to condemnations when they fail. Too often, the child's achievements are viewed as an indication of the worth of his or her parents, and failure brings reprisals based on the parents' feelings that they are to blame or that they themselves are inadequate. For many children, love becomes a premium handed out on the basis of what a child can *do* rather than simply on who he or she *is*.

The fastest and easiest way to create fear of failure in a child is to punish unsuccessful performance by criticizing it or by withholding love from the youngster. Under such circumstances, children learn to dread failure because it is associated with punishment or rejection. They also learn to fear and avoid situations in which they might fail. The unfortunate lesson they learn is that their worth and lovability depend on how well they perform. Instead of trying to achieve in order to reap the built-in rewards of achievement and mastery, children strive to perform well to avoid failure. They begin to measure themselves by their performance; and if their performance is inadequate, they usually consider their total being inadequate. Former UCLA basketball coach John Wooden has found that "Because they fear failure, many people never try and thereby rob themselves of opportunities to be successful."

Fear of failure is easy to create, but hard to get rid of because it is reinforced by widely accepted cultural beliefs.

As a parent, you can have a dramatic impact on helping the young athlete develop a positive desire to achieve rather than a fear of failure. Earlier, we described four elements in the stress cycle: (a) the situation, (b) mental appraisal of the situation, (c) physical arousal, and (d) coping behaviors. Efforts to reduce stress and build mental toughness can be directed at all four of these levels.

Reducing Situational Stress

The first way in which stress can be reduced is to change aspects of the situation that place unnecessary demands on young athletes. We are all well aware that coaches and parents can create stress by their actions. Many young athletes experience unnecessary stress because adults put undue pressure on them to perform well. Coaches who are punishing and abusive to children can create a very stressful and unenjoyable environment. Similarly, parents who yell at their children during games or withdraw their love if the young athlete lets them down can create a situation in which the youngster "runs scared" much of the time. Eliminating such actions by coaches and parents can reduce unnecessary stress.

Coaches enter into the life of a child for a limited period of time. But they occupy a central and critical role in youth sports and greatly influence the outcome of participation. Because of their key position, much of our research has focused on the psychological relationship between coaches and their athletes. As a result of a seven-year project, we developed a series of behavioral guidelines that proved effective in helping coaches to establish an enjoyable athletic environment. The guidelines are simply a set of principles that increase the ability to positively influence others, and they can help to reduce stress.

The *positive approach* emphasized in the coaching guidelines is specifically designed to counteract the conditions that create fear of failure. The same is true of the philosophy of winning discussed in Chapter 1. By promoting this philosophy of winning through use of the behavioral guidelines, coaches stand an excellent chance of creating a competitive sport environment in which children can enjoy themselves, develop their skills in an atmosphere of encouragement and reinforcement, and experience positive and supportive relationships with their coach and teammates.

**Coaches can be either a source of stress or a buffer
against its harmful effects.**

One of the most important differences between a positive approach to coaching and a negative approach is the kind of motivation that each produces. In a negative approach, punishment and criticism are used liberally in an attempt to "stamp out" mistakes. This approach operates by creating fear of failing. In contrast, the positive approach makes use of encouragement and reinforcement in an attempt to strengthen desirable behaviors. The motivation this kind of an approach develops is a positive desire to achieve and succeed rather than a negative fear of making mistakes. Thus, while both approaches may result in improvements in performance, they do so for different reasons and they create different types of *motivation*.

Under the positive approach, athletes come to see successful performance as an opportunity to experience a reward. On the other hand, the athlete who has been coached by the negative approach comes to view successful performance as a way of avoiding punishment. It is not surprising that athletes coached with a positive approach come to see pressure situations as challenges and opportunities, whereas those subjected to a negative approach see the same kinds of situations as threats. A discussion of the principles comprising the positive approach is presented in a book entitled *Handbook for Youth Sports Coaches*. (For pricing and order information, contact: American Alliance Publications, 1900 Association Drive, Reston, VA 22091; telephone (703) 476-3481.)

Increasing the Athlete's Resources: Skills and Social Support

Stress is experienced when we perceive an imbalance between the demands of the situation and the resources that we have to cope with the demands. It follows that another approach to reducing stress is to increase the young athlete's resources. Two types of resources are very important: (a) the skills that the athlete possesses, and (b) the amount of support that the athlete receives from important people, such as the coach, teammates, and parents. Parents and coaches are in a position to influence both types of resources.

It is quite natural to feel insecure when we don't have the skills needed to cope with a situation. Many young athletes experience this insecurity when they first begin to learn a sport. As their athletic skills increase, they become better able to deal with the demands of the athletic situation, and their stress decreases. Thus, being an effective teacher and working with your child to improve skills is one way that you can help reduce athletic stress. Here, again, we strongly recommend the positive approach, since we feel this is the most effective way to teach skills and create a positive learning environment. As athletes become more confident in their abilities, they see themselves as more prepared to cope with the demands of the athletic situation.

Athletic stress can be reduced by mastery of sport skills and by ample social support.

As a parent, you obviously are a potent source of social support for your child. But our research also shows quite clearly that coaches who use the positive approach have more cohesive teams on which athletes like one another more. By using their "reinforcement power" to encourage teammates to support one another, coaches can help create a higher level of social support for all of their athletes. When a team can pull together and support one another in pressure situations, this kind of social support can help reduce the level of stress experienced by individual athletes.

Coaches—and parents—can reduce stress by being supportive of young athletes.

Developing Winning Attitudes Toward Competition

Earlier, we noted that we use the term *stress* in two different ways. One use of the term relates to *situations* that place high demands on us. The other refers to our *response* to such situations. The importance of this distinction becomes particularly clear when we deal with the role of mental processes in stress. There is a big difference between *pressure situations* and *feeling pressure*. Mentally tough athletes perform well in pressure situations precisely because they have eliminated the pressure. They report that although intellectually they are aware that they are in a very tough situation, they really don't feel the *pressure* on the inside. There is no way to eliminate pressure *situations*; they will always be there because they are a natural part of competition. This does not mean, however, that athletes have to respond to such situations by experiencing high levels of stress and getting "psyched out."

Mentally tough competitors manage pressure well largely because they have become disciplined thinkers. Either consciously or unconsciously, they have made the connection in their own heads between what they think and how much pressure they feel during competition. They have learned (often the hard way) that thoughts like these produce pressure:

negative thinking

- What if I don't do well?

- I can't blow it now.

- I can't stand this pressure.

- I'll never live it down if I lose.

- If I miss these free throws, what will everyone say?

- If I don't sink this putt, I'll lose everything!

On the other hand, mentally tough athletes think like this in pressure situations:

- I'm going to do the best I can and let the cards fall where they may.

- All I can do is give 100 percent. No one can do more.

- This is supposed to be fun, and I'm going to make sure it is.

- • I don't have to put pressure on myself. All I have to do is focus on doing my job the best I know how.

- • I'm concentrating on performing rather than on winning or losing.

The first set of statements causes an athlete to react to adversity with stress and anxiety. The second set of statements focuses attention where it should be: on giving maximum effort and concentrating totally on what has to be done. Pressure situations become welcome opportunities, rather than dire threats, for mentally tough athletes. Former Marquette University basketball coach Al McGuire has said, "When an athlete can start loving adversity, I know I've got a competitor!" The bottom line is that the fundamental difference between mentally tough athletes and "chokers" is the way they choose to construct the situation in their heads. Situations are not nervous, tense, or anxious—people are! The sooner you can help athletes to realize that pressure comes from within and not from outside, the sooner they can start shutting it down.

One of the great benefits of sport as a training ground for mental toughness is that the consequences of failure are temporary and unlikely to have a long-term impact on the future of a child (as failing in school might). This places you in a great position to help your young athlete develop a healthy philosophy about achievement and an ability to tolerate failure and setbacks when they occur. The starting point for such training is the philosophy that great coaches like John Wooden and Vince Lombardi instilled in their athletes. We have described this philosophy in Chapter 1. These coaches developed mentally tough athletes and teams by realizing that an obsession with winning is self-defeating, because it places the cart before the horse. They realized that effort should be directed not toward winning, but toward performing to the very best of the athlete's ability at the time. Doing the very best one can at any moment should always be the focus and the goal. Winning will take care of itself; the only thing that can be directly controlled is *effort*. Mental toughness arises in the realization that "I am performing against myself, not someone else. I will always be my own toughest opponent, and winning the battle with myself paves the way for winning the contest with my opponent."

Here are some specific attitudes that you can communicate to your child.

1. Sports should be fun. Emphasize to your young athlete that sports and other activities in life are enjoyable for the playing, whether you win or lose. Athletes should be participating, first and foremost, to have fun. Try to raise your child to enjoy many activities in and of themselves so that winning is not a condition for enjoyment.

2. Anything worth achieving is rarely easy. There is nothing disgraceful about it being a long and difficult process to master something. Becoming the best athlete one can be is not an achievement to be had merely for the asking. Practice, practice, and still more practice is needed to master any sport.

"The will to win is important, but the will to prepare to win is essential."
Joe Paterno, college football coach

---

3. Mistakes are a necessary part of learning anything well. Very simply, if we don't make mistakes, we probably won't learn. Emphasize to your child that mistakes, rather than being things to avoid at all costs, are stepping stones to success. They give us the information we need to adjust and improve. The only true mistake is a failure to learn from our mistakes.

4. Effort is what counts. Emphasize and praise effort as well as outcome. Communicate repeatedly to your young athlete that all you ask is that he or she give total effort. Through your actions and your words, show your child that he or she is just as important to you when trying and failing as when succeeding. If maximum effort is acceptable to you, it can also become acceptable to your young athlete. Above all, do not punish or withdraw love and approval when he or she doesn't perform up to expectations. It is such punishment that builds fear of failure.

5. Do not confuse worth with performance. Help youngsters to distinguish what they do from what they are. A valuable lesson for children to learn is that they should never identify their worth as people with any particular part of themselves, such as their competence in sports, their school performance, or their physical appearance. You can further this process by demonstrating your own ability to accept your child unconditionally as a person, even when you are communicating that you don't approve of some behavior.

Also, show your child that you can gracefully accept your own mistakes and failures. Show and tell your child that as a fallible human being, you can accept the fact that despite your best efforts, you are going to occasionally bungle things. If children can learn to accept and like themselves, they will not unduly require the approval of others in order to feel worthwhile.

6. Pressure is something you put on yourself. Help your young athlete to see competitive situations as exciting self-challenges rather than as threats. Emphasize that he or she can choose how to think about pressure situations. The above attitudes will help to develop an outlook on pressure that transforms it into a challenge and an opportunity to test themselves and to achieve something worthwhile.

"The real competitor relishes the toughest situations. He doesn't have a choke level—he has an enjoyment level. He knows few players get to compete for the biggest rewards, and he loves it."
Johnny Majors, college football coach

---

7. Try to like and respect sport opponents. Some coaches and athletes think that proper motivation comes from anger or hatred for the opponent. We disagree. Sports should promote sportsmanship and an appreciation that opponents, far from being the "enemy," are fellow athletes who make it possible to compete. Hatred can only breed stress and fear. In terms of emotional arousal, fear and anger are indistinguishable patterns of physiologic responses. Thus, the arousal of anger can become the arousal of fear if things begin to go badly during a contest. College football coach Tom Osborne preaches respect for the opponent because, in his experience, "Athletes who play in a generally relaxed environment where there's goodwill toward their opponents are less fearful and play better."

When children learn to enjoy sports for their own sake, when their goal becomes to *do their best* rather than to *be the best*, and when they avoid the trap of defining their self-worth in terms of their performance or the approval of others, then their way of viewing themselves and their world is one that helps prevent stress. Such children are success-oriented rather than failure-avoidant. Parents who impart these lessons to their young athletes give them a priceless gift that will benefit them in many of their endeavors in life.

Controlling Arousal:
Teaching Your Child Relaxation Skills

Without carefully examining our thought processes, we may have little awareness of the appraisals that we are making about situations that produce stress. But we are all painfully aware of the physical responses of our bodies to such appraisals. We respond to perceived threat by shifting into high gear on a physiological level. Our heartbeat becomes faster and stronger so that more oxygen can be pumped through our bloodstream to the muscles. Our muscles become tense in readiness to confront the emergency. Stress hormones pouring into our bloodstream increase our level of arousal. These and other physiological changes are experienced by us as the stirred-up state that we associate with emotion. As noted earlier, a moderate level of arousal can psych us up to perform more efficiently. On the other hand, high levels of arousal can interfere with our thought and behavior patterns.

Arousal can be controlled with relaxation training.

The ability to remain calm in a stressful situation, or at least to prevent arousal from climbing out of control, is a useful stress management skill. Many athletes have found that they can learn to prevent or control high levels of tension through training in muscle relaxation skills. Because one cannot be relaxed and tense at the same time, voluntary relaxation gives athletes the ability to turn off or tone down tension. Although it is clearly a skill and must be learned through work and practice, most people can be trained to relax.

Relaxation training actually has two benefits. The first is the ability to reduce or control the level of arousal, but the second is equally important. In the course of relaxation training, people become more sensitive to what is going on inside their bodies and are better able to detect arousal in its beginning stages. When they can detect the early warning signs of developing tension, they can plug in their coping responses at an early stage before the tension gets out of control.

We have been training athletes in relaxation skills for many years. We have found that children as young as five or six years of age can be trained in relaxation, and they can then use these skills to reduce tension and anxiety. Our experience has been that children who learn this and other stress-coping skills (such as the attitudes described earlier) show a marked increase in self-confidence and are less reluctant to tackle difficult situations.

Mastering coping skills at an early age can benefit a child throughout life.

We now describe a training program that you can use to train your athletes (and yourself, if you wish) in relaxation skills. The approach that we describe involves training through a process of voluntarily tensing and relaxing various muscle groups. The goal is to learn voluntary relaxation skills while gaining increased sensitivity to body tension. We find that within about a week of conscientious training, most people can increase their ability to relax themselves and reduce tension.

If you wish to help your young athlete learn relaxation, we recommend that you go through the exercises on your own several times to become familiar with the procedure. Then you can easily guide your youngster through the exercises until they become familiar enough with them to practice without your help.

We recommend that the relaxation exercises be practiced at least once and preferably twice a day until they are mastered. Practice should be carried out in a comfortable chair or on a fairly soft floor (that is, on a carpeted floor or gym mat).

Explain to your child the reasons for relaxation training, and point out that many champion athletes have learned this skill. As you guide your youngster through the exercises, use a slow, relaxed tone of voice. Give the child plenty of time to experience the sensations, and make sure that he or she is doing the breathing part of the exercises correctly. The goal of the training is to combine relaxation, exhalation, and the mental command to relax repeatedly so that your young athlete will be able to induce relaxation by exhaling and mentally telling himself or herself to relax.

Mentally tough athletes have the ability to relax themselves quickly, even in the heat of competition.

In our training procedure, we start by concentrating on the hands and arms; move to the legs, stomach and chest, back muscles, and neck and jaw; and finish up with the facial and scalp muscles. Here are the steps.

Performance in precision sports like figure skating can be negatively affected by muscle tension.

1. While sitting comfortably, bend your arms at the elbow. Now make a hard fist with both hands, and bend your wrists downward while simultaneously tensing the muscles of your upper arms. This will produce a state of tension in your hands, forearms, and upper arms. Hold this tension for five seconds and study it carefully, then slowly let the tension out halfway while concentrating on the sensations in your arms and fingers as tension decreases. Hold the tension at the halfway point for five seconds, and then slowly let the tension out the rest of the way and rest your arms comfortably in your lap.

Concentrate carefully on the contrast between the tension which you have just experienced and the relaxation which deepens as you voluntarily relax the muscles for an additional ten to fifteen seconds. As you breathe normally, concentrate on those muscles and give yourself the mental command to relax each time you exhale. Do this for seven to ten breaths. If you train your young athlete, here is a sample of how you can phrase the instructions when presenting this exercise:

We're going to start out with the arms and hands. What I'd like you to do while keeping your eyes closed is to bend your arms and make a fist like this. [Demonstrate] Now make a hard fist and tense those muscles in your arms hard. Notice the tension and the pulling throughout your arms as those muscles stretch and bunch up like rubber bands. Focus on those feelings of tension in your arms and hands.

[After five seconds]: Now slowly begin to let that tension out halfway, and concentrate very carefully on the feelings in your arms and hands as you do that. Now hold the tension at the halfway point and notice how your arms and hands are less tense than before but that there is still tension present.

[After five seconds]: Now slowly let the tension out all the way and just let your arms and hands become completely relaxed, just letting go and becoming more and more relaxed, feeling all the tension draining away as the muscles let go and become completely relaxed. And now, each time you breathe out, let your mind tell your body to relax, and concentrate on relaxing the muscles even more. That's good . . . just let go.

2. Tense the calf and thigh muscles in your legs. You can do this by straightening out your legs hard while pointing your toes downward. Hold the tension for five seconds, then slowly let it out halfway. Hold the halfway point for an additional five seconds, and then slowly let the tension out all the way and concentrate on relaxing the muscles as completely as possible. Again, pay careful attention to the feelings of tension and relaxation as they develop. Finish by giving the muscles the mental command "Relax" each time you exhale (seven to ten times), and concentrate on relaxing them as deeply as possible.

3. Cross the palms of your hands in front of your chest and press them together to tense the chest and shoulder muscles. At the same time, tense your stomach muscles hard. As before, hold the tension for five seconds, then slowly let the tension out halfway and focus on the decreasing levels of tension as you

do so. Hold again for five seconds at the halfway point and then slowly let the tension out completely. Again, do the breathing procedure with the mental command to deepen the relaxation in your stomach, chest, and shoulder muscles.

4. Arch your back and push your shoulders back as far as possible to tense your upper and lower back muscles. (Be careful not to tense these muscles too hard.) Repeat the standard procedure of slowly releasing the tension halfway, then all the way. Finish by doing the breathing exercise and mental command as you relax your back muscles as deeply as possible.

5. Tense your neck and jaw muscles by thrusting your jaw outward and drawing the corners of your mouth back. Release the tension slowly to the halfway point, hold for five seconds there, and then slowly release the tension in these muscles all the way. Let your head droop into a comfortable position and your jaw slacken as you concentrate on totally relaxing these muscles with your breathing exercise and mental command. (You can also tense your neck muscles in other ways, such as bending your neck forward, backward, or to one side. Experiment to find out the way that's best for you. Tense your jaw at the same time.)

6. Wrinkle your forehead and scalp to tense these muscles. Hold the tension for five seconds, then release it halfway for an additional five seconds. Then relax your eyes completely. Focus on relaxing your facial and scalp muscles completely, and use your breathing exercise and mental command.

7. While sitting in a totally relaxed position, take a series of short inhalations, about one per second, until your chest is filled and tense. Hold each for about five seconds, then exhale slowly while thinking silently to yourself, "Relax." Most people can produce a deeply relaxed state by doing this. Repeat this exercise three times.

8. Finish off your relaxation practice by concentrating on breathing comfortably into your abdomen (rather than into your chest area). Simply let your stomach fill with air as you inhale, and deepen your relaxation as you exhale. Abdominal breathing is far more relaxing than breathing into the chest.

As you guide your young athlete through the exercises, you can practice them yourself. You will find relaxation very useful in your own life. It not only serves as a weapon against tension and stress, but it produces an enjoyable state in its own right.

Urge your child to use relaxation skills whenever he or she begins to feel unduly tense. Relaxation can also be used for preparing to deal with stressful situations by imagining these situations while concentrating on remaining completely relaxed. For example, the young athlete might imagine shooting a crucial free throw in a basketball game as vividly as possible while maintaining as deep a state of relaxation as possible. Relaxation together with mental rehearsal is a technique used by many champion athletes as part of their mental preparations for stressful athletic situations. We have found that child athletes can also benefit from this procedure.

The stresses of athletic competition must be faced by all athletes, young and old. As a parent, you can use these stresses as opportunities to teach your youngster coping skills that will be beneficial not only in sports but in other areas of life as well. The athlete's greatest enemy is fear of failure, and anything that you can do to prevent this from developing or to teach your youngster to master it will help to make sport participation more enjoyable and productive.

CHAPTER 8

CHAPTER 8
MALE AND FEMALE
HIGH SCHOOL ATHLETES:
Drugs, College Recruiting,
and Other Concerns

Recently, a former All-American football player sat in the stands with his elderly father, watching his son play in a state championship football game. In the middle of the third quarter, the son took the ball and ran through the opposition eighty-two yards for what was to be the winning touchdown. As the shouting and cheering died, the grandfather turned to his son, the former All-American player, and proclaimed, "You have now had your greatest experience in sport." Having watched his son perform similar sport heroics a generation earlier, the grandfather knew whereof he spoke.

It is obviously gratifying to watch our sons and daughters perform well. They will not all win championship games; many won't make the starting team, but we hope that most school districts will provide an opportunity for all to participate. Sport participation at this age is fun and provides opportunities for self-confidence, acceptance by peers and adults, and fitness.

If sports are all that good at this age, then what are the problems? Many of the issues discussed in previous chapters apply in a special way to high school-aged athletes. We explore a few in this chapter in the hope that we may help make the high school sport experience just a little bit better.

The Young Woman Athlete in High School

The high school female in sports are a relatively new phenomenon. Competing in a physical, demanding activity for the first time, the young woman with little sport experience may encounter problems in knowing when to press ahead, when to go all out, and when to take it a bit easy. She may have no understanding of how important it is to pace herself during early workouts and practices. Few things can take the joy out of sports more effectively than over-exertion when one is not properly conditioned for an all-out effort.

The need for preseason conditioning may be overlooked by the "new" young woman athlete.

A female high school athlete should start a conditioning pro-gram with her friends before the season begins. She should be ready for that day when the coach suggests some intense efforts to see "who really wants to be on the team." Starting six to eight weeks before the season to do some stretching, strengthening, and aero-bic conditioning exercises with a small group of peers can be fun. It will assure them all a better chance of keeping up when they do turn out for the team.

Even in self-directed preseason exercise, the new athlete may have to be reminded not to exercise when she has pain and, if some joint or tendon area begins to hurt, to ease up and give it some rest. Don't let the young woman believe that playing through pain is a smart part of sports. When it hurts you, you're hurting it!

Parents should be prepared for the time when their athlete daughter begins to take her sport experience seriously. Women's sports in high school are providing opportunities of the same degree of intensity and commitment as have been available to young men.

Academic, extracurricular, and social activities should not and need not be forgotten or sacrificed for a high school sport career.

The day has arrived for young women in high school sports when a superstar can emerge, attracting all the attention and adu-lation that have come to select male athletes in the past. With all of this can come some exciting days for the parents and some very real responsibilities. If your household is blessed with a young woman high school superstar, be sure her sport activity doesn't un-duly rule your household and everyone in it. Learn about the col-lege recruiting process before it starts and get an unbiased appraisal by a respected college coach as to just how much poten-tial your young athlete has in the world of collegiate women sports. Most importantly, keep a close eye on those report cards and take advantage of opportunities to introduce some interest into the family life other than sports.

Some Sport Concerns for Young Women Only

Menstruation

With the marked increase in sport participation by young women, there is a very natural concern about the effect of menstruation on sport performance as well as about the impact of intense competition and training on a young woman's reproductive cycle. Limited studies to date suggest that with the exception of elite swimmers, the age of menarche (the onset of the menstrual period) is later in women athletes than in nonathletes. A study of

The needs of the female athlete deserve special attention.

145 female athletes at the Montreal Olympic Games found that the average age of onset of menses was 13.7 years and that women athletes had a later onset than did the general population of their country of origin. Runners and gymnasts as groups had the latest onset—14.3 and 14.5 years—and swimmers had the earliest, 13.1 years. In another investigation, the onset of menstruation was found to be 14.2 years in a group of Olympic volleyball players, 13 years in high school and college athletes, and 12.2 years in a matched population of nonathletes.

The reason for the delayed onset of menstruation in athletes is not well defined and doubtless varies in different populations of women. In some, the stress of intense training and competition at an early age may delay the onset of menstruation. In others, such as gymnasts and long-distance runners, the marked reduction in the level of body fat for elite performance could be a factor. In sports such as basketball and volleyball, very tall girls become elite performers. To attain an extremely tall height, most girls experience a prolonged period of preadolescent growth and are late maturers. The late onset of menstruation is part of their slower-than-average maturation process.

The relation of menstrual flow to sport performance has been investigated in several populations of elite athletes. Olympic gold medals have been won by women during every phase of the menstrual cycle. Elite athletes report that they train and compete without difficulty during and between periods. For whatever reason, disabling menstrual-related discomfort is less common in athletes. Dealing with menstrual discomfort in sport performance, training, and competing depends on the severity of the pain and the degree of commitment of the young woman to her sport program. A physician can prescribe medications that are quite effective in providing symptomatic relief for the discomfort experienced by many and that will permit continued training or competition. If the discomfort makes sport participation painful and unpleasant, the young female athlete should remain on the sidelines temporarily. It isn't necessary to prove anything by ignoring the body's signals.

Although there are fewer problems of menstrual irregularity and discomfort among athletes than nonathletes, the incidence of missed periods and the cessation of the menstrual cycle for prolonged periods occur commonly in populations of women athletes who are involved in intense training. Those young women most likely to experience missed periods and interruption of the normal menstrual cycle include (a) distance runners and other endurance athletes who experience marked reductions in their level of body fat, (b) those making a very keen commitment to a given period of training, (c) those who had a late menarche, and (d) any girls who experienced irregular menstrual periods before beginning sport participation and training.

The long-term effects of irregular menstrual cycles and missed periods on women's health and reproductive capacity are not known.

Anecdotal reports of several elite athletes who have experienced altered menstrual function with training and sport participation but normal pregnancies suggest that there is no evidence of any decreased fertility. Women athletes reportedly experience fewer complications of pregnancy, fewer Caesarean sections, shorter duration of labor, and fewer spontaneous abortions; this is not an unexpected reproductive record for a population of very fit women. For the young female athlete who is intensely involved in sport and is experiencing irregular menstrual periods, prolonged periods, or absence of menstrual cycles, a visit to the gynecologist is strongly recommended.

Equipment Needs of the Female Athlete

With the wonderful expansion in the number of women and girls participating in sports and the great variation in the sports they are involved in, there are certain needs for better equipment for the female athlete. In most situations, female sports equipment, such as shoes, socks, shorts, pants, sweatshirts, and jerseys, is no different from that of the male athlete. All equipment should be clean and in good repair and should fit properly. This is obviously of considerable importance in regard to footwear. Proper-fitting jerseys can become important if there is underlying protective padding that must be held in place by a good-fitting jersey.

Hot weather presents a unique challenge to the woman athlete who can't go topless to expose as much heat-radiating skin as her male counterpart can. Cutoffs—half-tops exposing the lower chest and upper abdomen—are appropriate pieces of equipment for distance runners and other athletes who may train and compete in warm and humid weather.

Attention must be given to the problem of support and protection of the female breast in vigorous sport activities.

Being a quite freely mobile fatty structure, the female breast is not very vulnerable to significant injury. Serious bruises requiring surgery have occurred in a few rare instances in which the breasts, firmly immobilized against the chest with a wide elastic bandage, received a strong blow. With excellent breast-support bras available for the active athlete, there is no reason to support and immobilize the breasts in this inappropriate manner. There is no evidence to suggest that bumps or bruises in a well-supported breast during athletic participation will have any relation to the eventual development of cancer or tumors.

Currently, a few well-designed bras for the female athlete are on the market. One bra that can be highly recommended was designed after very sophisticated biomechanical research by a group of investigators headed by Christine Haycock, a distinguished surgeon and accomplished athlete. This bra, marketed as the Lady Duke, provides excellent support for the breast and can even be padded for protection in sports in which padding may be desired. Good support of the breasts during active body movements is essential for comfort and good performance.

The female athlete may pursue sports that warrant attention to special equipment. Some sports require strength training which may involve popular pieces of equipment that have been designed for use by adult males. Young males and most females do not fit these pieces of training equipment and should use them with discretion if injuries and overuse problems are to be avoided. Also, some athletes exercise on seats designed for use by males. The dimensions of the pelvic bones on which women sit differ greatly from men's. The seats of racing or touring bicycles, of racing shells, and of white-water kayaks all may be sources of considerable discomfort to the female athlete. Seats designed for women in these sports can be specially ordered. They provide a good bit of comfort to the female and improve her performance.

Supporting Disengagement from Intense Involvement

Prior to high school, athletics for some girls has meant an intense involvement in gymnastics, figure skating, synchronized swimming, or swim racing. The preadolescent and early-adolescent girl willingly accepts the discipline and demanding training programs of these sports, enjoying the gratifying attention of coaches and parents. As she reaches high school age, her social horizons suddenly broaden and the young man across the aisle in homeroom isn't quite the irritation he was the year before. Life begins to provide interesting alternatives to five or six hours a day in the gym or at the swimming pool. The young woman athlete may quite suddenly begin to underperform and put on ten pounds of fat that she can't seem to lose.

Painful as it is to accept, it is probably the end of the line. Your Olympic hopeful has had enough. Regardless of the thousands of dollars spent on lessons, fees, medical bills, and trips to competitions over the years, Mom and Dad will do well to prepare themselves to accept some new accomplishments and enjoyments of their young athlete. These talented girls who have been heavily committed to and quite successful in the sports commonly practiced by preadolescent girls often are quite disinterested in team sports in high school. They may have had enough of gyms, swimming pools, and coaches, and find it a bit dull to play with less-talented, "average" high school athletes. A recent study of adult women who had been elite competitive swimmers as young girls found that after they left their very demanding swim programs, they shunned active sports and as adults were much less active than women who had never made a serious commitment to sports as young girls.

Be certain that the door leading out of intense sport involvement can be easily opened by a young woman athlete who has had enough.

The Early- and Late-Maturing Male Athlete

A large number of the disappointments and problems that surround sport participation at the high school level relate to the involvement in sports by young men who are maturing at a pace that differs from the average. The implications of these maturation differences were discussed in Chapter 3 and present very real concerns in men's sports, where the ability to compete is often related to size, strength, and the level of physical maturity. Because of the special relevance of this issue to high school youngsters, the major points bear repeating here.

The early-maturing male, who has experienced rapid growth in height in the sixth or seventh grade, is shaving occasionally as he starts high school, and is well-muscled before he leaves junior high school, can be enjoying outstanding athletic success in youth sport programs and on junior high school teams. He has been a year or two more mature than his teammates who are of the same chronologic age. During high school, his teammates begin to catch up in maturation and most will soon attain greater size and strength. No longer stronger or bigger than most of his peers, he must face what will be a painful and difficult adjustment to a less stellar role in sports. He has been a star performer because of his early physical maturity and not because of any unique skill or talent. This young man can be directed to sport participation where size and strength are not major determinants of sport proficiency, and he can be encouraged to become involved in some rewarding activities outside sport participation.

For the early-maturing "all star," arrange sport competition with individuals of the same maturing status rather than limiting participation to those of the same chronologic age.

Preventing high school disappointments that can be distressful for parent and athlete alike may be accomplished during the junior high school years. The outstanding eighth-grade basketball forward might work out with the high school junior varsity and thus keep his true athletic talent potential in realistic perspective. The early-maturing fourteen-year-old tennis champion should play some matches with the sixteen-year-olds to help him understand whether or not he'll continue to excel.

Frustration and disappointment of another kind is in store for the slow, delayed maturer, the young man whose growth and physical development occur after the rest of his classmates are well on their way to being physically grown-up. If the later maturer is small (and most, but not all, are), he won't be competitive in most sports because of his size. In wrestling, even though matched in competition on a weight basis, the small later maturer will not do well because of lack of strength and endurance. The small late maturer may find a positive experience in the racket sports or running sports. Even if he is a tall, large, late-maturing boy, he won't have the strength or potential for endurance that will allow him to play up to expectation for someone of his size. Even in sports where strength is not a major determinant of performance, the late maturer will probably have problems due to lack of endurance.

Reassurance is needed by these boys and is best provided by a sensitive physician who can inform the young man and his concerned parents about the normal progression of maturation changes and the individual's timetable for acquiring increased strength and size. If maturation is markedly delayed, an endocrinologist might recommend endocrine treatment to hasten the maturation process.

Drugs and the High School Athlete

A host of drugs are available to high school students on the street and in the school. How does drug abuse relate to newly expanding sport participation by today's student population? Perhaps drug experimentation among those high school students in sport programs is little different from experimentation among the members of the student body in general. However, young men and women who have serious problems with drug abuse are not commonly involved in school sports.

The young person freaked out on drugs is not going to be very competitive on any sport team.

There are other reasons why the street-drug problem isn't often found in the high school locker room. Participation in a high school athletic program can provide a young man or woman athlete with a very good reason to avoid drug abuse and may give some very practical alternative highs. It puts him or her in an environment where drug abuse isn't, and can't be, "cool." Another reason is that drug use interferes with athletic performance and serious abuse is readily recognized. If a troubled young athlete begins to show some unexplained changes in behavior and a real drug problem is identified, coaches and parents alike must face the issue and, in a nonjudgmental and supportive manner, get the athlete qualified, comprehensive treatment. *There are no minor drug problems among high school students.*

Although the athlete may be at less risk of abusive use of street drugs, there are a host of sport-related drug abuses that parents, athletes, and coaches must be alert to and be prepared to deal with. Over the years a large number of chemical agents have found their way into sports, supposedly to increase the athletic prowess of the user. To date there has not been a single agent among the thousands of chemicals and drugs available that can be demonstrated to increase the athletic performance of a healthy athlete. Currently, there are two drugs commonly found in the locker room that present very real dangers. Both have been around long enough to have been studied under rigidly controlled conditions and found to have no significant effect on performance in sports. These are amphetamines ("speed") and anabolic steroids, or male sex hormones.

Amphetamines, although more common on the sport scene a few years ago than today, are still around. They are powerful nervous-system stimulants. They give the athlete an exaggerated sense of performance, reduce powers of perception, alter fine coordination, and increase the risk of injury. The altered, hyped-up, and inappropriate agitation of the amphetamine user usually make the speed freak obvious in the pregame locker room. Any user will need some information and counseling. Further steps may be required if the amphetamines are being provided by a misguided parent or coach.

Anabolic steroids (synthetic male hormones) are particularly attractive these days to young men in football, the so-called strength sports, and certain field events, such as the shot put and discus throw. The young man trying to increase body weight and muscle mass with a program of increased food intake and weight training will sooner or later encounter some "gym rat" who has hormone capsules or injections that are alleged to really "put on" the muscle. These drugs will increase size and appearance of

Drugs, vitamins, and food supplements can be a threat to the well-being of the high school athlete.

muscles for a short time. This increase in muscle size is of brief duration and is due only to water retention in the muscle. This form of drug abuse is common among competitive body builders. The doses often used are so dangerous that it is unethical to study their effects systematically.

These substances do not solve the problem of body weight and muscle mass. In fact, they do not increase muscle mass in a healthy young man. Nature has provided him with the ability to produce all of the male hormones he can use.

Anabolic steroids will, in the long run, take their harmful toll.

Over time, the presence of anabolic steroids turns off the production of the male's own hormones and causes shrinkage of the testicles, which produce these hormones. Taking anabolic steroids over a long time can result in scarring of the testicles and permanent sterility. These drugs are not only useless and dangerous but flagrantly unethical. They have no place in sports.

Sickness and Injury

As a group, high school athletes are the healthiest members of a very healthy segment of the population. They can, however, encounter minor illnesses brought on by nonspecific respiratory infections, such as colds and flu. To a competitive high school athlete, however, there are no such things as minor illnesses. *An athlete with a fever should not practice, work out, or play without a physician's examination and clearance.* Fever responses to illness vary a good bit among individuals, but as a general rule, a fever of 100 degrees or greater should put an athlete on the sidelines. Not only will an athlete with a fever play poorly (regardless of all protests to the contrary), he or she will expose other teammates to the infection. There is also a very remote possibility of the cold or flu virus affecting heart muscle so that it won't tolerate the stress of vigorous exercise. Even the finest body can use a little help with rest in combating an infection. That will help make the illness as brief as possible.

On rare occasions the high school-aged athlete can be laid low with something more serious than a common cold or nonspecific viral infection. Infectious mononucleosis or severe streptococcal pharyngitis (strep throat) can put the young athlete in bed for a week or more. Coming back from such a setback can be demanding and frustrating. The athlete will need all the support and understanding he or she can get from parents, teammates, and the coach.

As a general rule, it will take at least three days of reconditioning for every day of illness and inactivity.

The infection that keeps the basketball starter in bed at home for a week may set him back in conditioning three weeks after he feels completely well. Getting back to training before he is completely well, free of fever, and able to go to school all day will only prolong his illness and the period of underperformance. Why the body responds in this way isn't well understood, but endurance and strength come back very slowly after a significant infection and enforced inactivity. The experience may be made a bit more tolerable if athletes know how long it is going to take to get back to pre-illness levels of performance.

The increased intensity of competition, the greater strength and size of athletes, and the greater periods of time high school athletes spend at sports all make sport injury a common part of high school sports. Elsewhere we have devoted a chapter to the nature and management of sport injuries. Parents should become familiar with that chapter and should share with their athletes information about how the athlete's minor injuries are to be managed at home. (There must be some very good reason for the high school athlete's common complaint that no one could know less about how to manage injuries than parents!) Together you should prepare an optimum treatment plan for minor sprains, strains, and contusions. Know how to effectively provide ICE treatment over the weekend to those hurts from a Friday night game. Have elastic bandages wet and refrigerated and plastic produce bags ready for crushed ice. Know how to elevate a bed to keep an injured ankle from swelling overnight. Have ice cups in your refrigerator to provide ice massage for minor overuse injuries that can be effectively treated during an evening.

Inadequately rehabilitated sport injuries are found throughout high school sports. Adequate rehabilitation of an injured ankle, knee, or shoulder is the greatest unmet need in the medical care of high school athletes. A weakened leg or arm puts an athlete at increased risk to another injury and obviously hurts performance. Following an injury, an arm or leg should be exercised until the strength and range of motion of joints are equal to those of the uninjured arm or leg. This degree of rehabilitation should be reached before the athlete attempts to return to practice or competition. Getting the athlete to the rehabilitation facility, providing specific exercise needs at home, and observing the youngster's progress are important contributions by parents to injury management.

An additional aspect of injury management, and one that may seem somewhat peripheral to the injury, is the maintenance of fitness during the period of recovery from a sport injury. In addition to the obvious need to stay fit for the most prompt and effective return to competition, the high school athlete needs some sport-related activity to occupy those hours that were previously given to athletic endeavors. The young man or woman with an injured arm can run and do lower-extremity weight training. The individual with a lower-extremity injury can soon begin to swim or work on upper-body weight training. Separating a previously busy high school student from friends still involved with the team is an invitation to some less-than-desirable activities. Coaches, busy with their teams, cannot be expected to fill these hours. Encouragement and support from home will often be needed.

Parents' responsibilities in injuries:
- **Be prepared for treatment at home.**
- **Be sure rehabilitation is complete.**
- **Encourage the athlete to stay fit.**

How to Handle College Recruiting

Soon after the turn of the century, when an Ivy League university constructed a stadium that would seat tens of thousands of spectators for the university's football games, collegiate sports became big business. They have continued to be so. If your son or daughter has had a truly outstanding high school sport career, he or she is going to be invited into this multibillion-dollar enterprise. He or she will be recruited.

For the high school athlete and his or her parents, recruiting can be a very positive culmination of a fine high school athletic career, or it can mean weeks of irritation, frustration, and anxiety, leading eventually to a much-regretted decision about the athlete's future education and athletic opportunity.

Playing the recruiting game demands a well-thought-out game plan. What follows are some guidelines to how the recruiting game is played and how to end up a winner.

- Know the rules. Don't try to play this game *without* knowing them.

- Know how good your athlete really is. How badly are people really going to want him or her in their program?

- Set down some guidelines and rules for dealing with recruiting in your own personal family situation. What are you going to allow and what is going to be off limits in your particular situation?

- Know as specifically as possible what your son or daughter really wants in a school. What kind of an academic program and school should it be, and where should it be located? What kind of sport program will your child be happiest in? These things should be well thought through before the recruiters are in the living room.

- Parents and athletes alike have to realize at the outset that they must be completely honest with themselves and the schools' representatives. Prolonging the attention and the courting may be a titillating game, but the athlete will end up the loser. Recruiters who are not dealt with in a reasonably straightforward way won't be misled. Your athlete isn't the first one they ever tried to entice to their school.

How Will Colleges and Universities Know About Your High School Athlete?

Intercollegiate sport is an intensely competitive activity, and one can feel quite confident that little of the talent that makes for winners is ever going to be overlooked. In spite of the instances in which eventual sport stars were overlooked (Bill Russell was recruited by only one school, and that one very near his hometown), true athletic talent at the high school level is not very apt to be bypassed. High school coaches get great satisfaction in bringing to the attention of college coaches their "well-coached" young stars. The college coaches, their assistants, former athletes, and other alumni all monitor high school sports in various geographic areas, on the lookout for the potential collegiate performer. In addition to these scouting efforts, there are highly efficient professional scouting services subscribed to by collegiate sport programs. They provide sophisticated, professional evaluations of high school athletes from all across the country. For an appropriate fee, these services give college coaches professional analyses of high school athletes who they observe in summer camps, preseason workouts, and actual competition wherever an outstanding high school athlete may perform. If your son or daughter has the potential to be a collegiate athlete, college coaches are very apt to know about it.

The first step: Learn the rules of the recruiting game.

Playing any game demands that the players know and abide by the rules. It is especially true in this recruiting game. Breaking the rules (and the easiest way to break the rules is not to know them) can cost your son or daughter a college athletic career and perhaps a college education.

At the first sign of college athletic recruitment, write for *The NCAA Guide for the College-Bound Student-Athlete* at the National

The search for potential college athletes is now a highly sophisticated process.

Collegiate Athletic Association, Nall Ave. at 63rd St., P.O. Box 1906, Mission, KS 66201. The young athlete and his or her parents should be familiar with the information in this pamphlet and should heed the statement on page 6 of the publication, which states: "Do not permit prospective student athletes to jeopardize their collegiate eligibility through involvement in violation of NCAA legislation."

How Good Is Your Athlete?
How Interested Are Colleges Going to Be?

It is essentially impossible for any of us as parents to be completely objective in appraising the real abilities and talents of our children. It is hoped that most of us perceive our offspring (regardless of intermittent evidence to the contrary) as sensational. The high school coach of your talented son or daughter may also lack objectivity. Yet it is important to get a reasonable measure of the young athlete's true potential and capacity to compete. One suggestion that has served as a good technique for several high school seniors is to seek out a nearby college or junior college coach at a school in which the athlete has no recruitment interest. Make arrangements to get that coach's professional appraisal of the athlete. In this way, at least one major question can be answered: Is the athlete physically big enough and quick enough to play competitively in college? Most high school competitions don't test these traits to the degree that they will be needed in college competition. The six-foot-five high school basketball player is going to be middle height in college basketball and may be a half-step too slow in the eyes of a college coach. It is best to know from the start any limitations your athlete might have and at what level of college competition he or she can play.

Establishing Some Recruiting Ground Rules
for You and Your Athlete

Before things go any further, some questions about handling recruiting are in order. Who will talk to the recruiters? How are you to decide whom to talk to? Whom will you allow to visit in your home? How are you to control the effects of these invasions on your athlete's school responsibilities and after-school life? How are you going to keep some balance with other family members' interests and priorities?

Some planning can eliminate much of the disruption and potential distress. First, some decisions should be made as to what the athlete sees as top priorities in his college experience.

- How important are prestigious academic opportunities, and in what general academic areas do your athlete's interests lie?

- How competitive is he or she academically?

- Does your athlete need academic assistance?

- Does the athlete feel strongly about staying close to home, or is there a sincere desire to go to some other part of the country?

- Will your athlete go anywhere for the right academic and/or sport program?

- What kind of sport program will the athlete be most successful and satisfied in?

- What style of play, coaching, and team personality will he or she find most satisfying?

Answering these questions early in the recruiting process may eliminate a large percentage of interested schools. It is not uncommon, if they have kept in close touch with the athlete's high school coach during these discussions, for the family and athlete to have the coach screen all the interested schools and their recruiters. The coach can determine which schools satisfy the criteria developed in earlier discussions. Probably no more than a half-dozen schools will be of real interest to even the most-sought-after high school star.

Much of the harassment of outstanding athletes and their families during the recruiting process has been eliminated by present-day NCAA legislation.

No recruiting is allowed during the active sport season in high school. The athlete is restricted in the number of colleges he or she can be invited to visit, and the number of visits is also regulated. The number of home contacts is limited as well.

Visits by recruiters are followed by visits to a limited number of campuses. These visits, of course, are highly structured sales pitches carefully orchestrated to impress the student athlete. He or she will have no problem getting to see that part of university or college life that is thought to appeal most. Students are shown the athletic facilities and they visit with the athletes—perhaps even eat at the training table—but they can spend no more than forty-eight hours at each campus visit.

Experienced coaches often gain a good deal of insight into the personality and maturity of the athlete during the on-campus visit. This social glimpse is an important part of the recruiting process for both parties. Is this big, quick athlete going to be a coachable team player? More than one young athlete has found a school's interest cooled or terminated after the on-campus visit.

The NCAA has legislation concerning high school academic-performance standards required for admission to varsity athletic programs in member colleges and universities. They are more stringent than in the past and are a sharp reminder to the talented high school athlete not to neglect high school scholastic responsibilities.

During the all-important senior year of high school, when sport performances can be truly outstanding and a heavy responsibility, academic matters cannot be ignored.

Sharing Concerns

Comments made by some of today's high school athletes can give us valuable insights into their concerns. Recently, high school athletes from a midwestern state participated in a series of open forums in which they, their coaches, and parents all had opportunities to talk about high school sports. Strong and widely varied opinions and feelings were expressed by parents, coaches, and student athletes alike. Here are some examples of the comments made:

Coach

- You ask me if soccer is a matter of life or death? No, it is more important than that!

Parents

- We question the constitutionality of rules which limit the length of seasons, practices, and training. We feel they are discriminatory, detrimental to the child, and an infringement of individual freedom. In our modern society it is unrealistic for any group to establish limits as to what extent any child may pursue his or her ambitions, and to do so would certainly kill initiative.

- I built a hockey rink in our backyard so my kids could practice every day. I figure I can save twenty thousand dollars in college costs and then they'll have a good shot at the pros.

High school athletes

- I wish there were rules that would set the amount of time I have to practice every day. I was in the pool at six o'clock this morning and I have to go back tonight and work out again. On Sundays I'm expected to find an open pool and practice all afternoon. Look at me, I'm tired and beat...and there's two months left to the high school season and then summer practice starts.

- In every contest someone loses. Athletes can accept that fact. Why can't adults? After all, what's wrong with third place?

- The worst part of athletics is having to go home after a game and listen to your dad tell you what you did wrong.

- I don't like a coach who cuts corners to win. One night my coach sent me in to get into a fight with the star player on the other team. We were both removed from the game. Our team only lost me. The other team lost their star. But you know, no one won that game that night.

- When I'm a bench warmer I don't want to be put into the game if it means we look bad.

- Don't drop the alcohol rule. Even though lots of athletes violate the rule, those who want to maintain high standards can tell their friends they can't drink because the rule is there.

- My parents never missed a game when my brother played hockey, but it took four years to get them to one of my gymnastics meets.

High school athletes did not like parents who:

- Hound you when you lose. I know some kids who have ulcers!

- Expect me to live up to the reputation of my brother or sister.
- Still wear their letter jackets.

High school athletes appreciated parents who

- Don't push me.
- Still like me even when my team loses.
- Let me choose any sport that I want to participate in.
- Took me to lots of games in all sports. I appreciated that.
- Give me encouragement and understanding. I need that.

Being a parent of a high school athlete can sometimes provide some of your greatest moments. Most certainly it will provide some of the real challenges. Nobody ever said that being a parent of an active growing young person was going to be dull, predictable, or easy. Remember that the goal of sports must always be, first and foremost, to have fun—for the high school participant and certainly for the parent, who can do no better than allow that high school youth to continue to grow up and away through experiences in sports.

CHAPTER 9

CHAPTER 9
SURVIVING YOUTH SPORTS:
A Commonsense Approach
to Some Challenging Issues

Before writing this book, we interviewed numerous parents, sport program administrators, coaches, and young athletes. We felt that their input and the kinds of questions and issues that they were grappling with needed to be covered. To give you some idea of the range of concerns that were expressed, here is a sampling of some of the comments we heard as sport psychology and sports medicine professionals:

I am worried about my son. He seems to have gotten things out of perspective as far as sports are concerned. Although he's only thirteen years old, he's convinced that his future lies in college and professional sports. Nothing else seems to matter.

For two years all my son has talked about is playing peewee football. He loves the game and watches the sport all the time on television. This year he finally was old enough to try out for a team. He just got cut and is really hurt. What can I do to cheer him up and show him there is a tomorrow?

I'm coaching a girls' softball team. My players are all average in ability, and some of them have relatively little talent. The problem I'm having is that every time we lose a game, their parents, in order to boost their morale, either blame it on poor coaching by me or on bad calls by the umpires. How can I get these kids to understand reality?

We screwed up and lost the state championship game. I'm so down and out that I'm ashamed to face anyone.

My kids are getting too big for their britches. We're undefeated and the kids are so overconfident that they're getting obnoxious. How can I bring them down to earth?

My son hardly ever gets into games. He likes to play, but he's not very good. It seems like he's going to spend the whole season as a bench warmer. He's talking about quitting. Should I let him or not?

My eldest son has never had much athletic talent. His younger brother is terrific and is really in the limelight. I can see that it's causing problems between them and that the older boy is having trouble dealing with his brother's success. I feel like I need to do something about it.

I went out to watch my son's wrestling practice the other night. I was amazed to see what the coach was doing and saying to those kids. He's a real animal with a foul mouth. I don't want Steve exposed to a coach like that unless he changes. What should I do?

I'm the president of a youth basketball league. We're not having any problems with the kids or coaches, but the parents are another matter. They're yelling at officials and at their own kids, and the games are getting to be a real circus. If things don't get better, we may have to do something drastic.

My husband and I thought that sports would bring the family closer together. Instead, we're chasing all over, and we see less and less of each other. We never do anything as a family anymore, and this has gotten to be a year-round thing. I'm starting to feel that Bob and I are growing farther apart.

Helping Put Athletics in Perspective for Your Child

In the preceding chapters we have shown how athletics can contribute to the personal, social, and physical well-being of youngsters. Sports are an important area in the lives of many youngsters, and for a small number, youth sports are the first phase of a journey that ends in a career in professional athletics. Perhaps you hope that your child is headed in this direction.

To strive for high standards of athletic excellence is commendable. But parents and athletes alike must realize that the chances of actually becoming a professional are remote. Even if your child appears to be a gifted athlete, the odds are overwhelming. The following table shows how selective the process is for football, basketball, and baseball. The figures for football show that only 1 in 6,666 high school football players will go on to play professional football. In basketball the corresponding figure is 1 in 14,000. And for baseball the statistics indicate that only 1 in 1,200 in the free-agent pool actually makes a major league team. Even the small number who rise to the world of professional sports can only count on a very short career. Football and basketball players typically last fewer than five years, and the average career of a major league baseball player is seven years.

The Odds Against Becoming a Professional Athlete

	Football	Basketball	Baseball
High School Seniors	1,000,000	700,000	
College Seniors	41,000	15,000	
Free-Agent Pool			120,000
Pro Draft Picks	320	200	1,200
Pro Teams	150	50	100
Odds	**1 in 6,666**	**1 in 14,000**	**1 in 1,200**

Given the reality of the situation, a career in professional sports or even participation at the college level is an unrealistic goal for the majority of young athletes. It is therefore important to impress upon youngsters that sports are but one part of their life. It is all too easy for youngsters and parents alike to harbor fantasies of turning pro and to sacrifice other areas of development in pursuit of that fabled status and its rewards of fame, money, and glory. It is not at all uncommon for athletes to become one-dimensional people.

College athletes commonly forsake educational opportunities, to their own later despair.

Many athletes view college as only preparation for their professional careers in sports. Schoolwork is seen as important only to maintain athletic eligibility. As a result, an alarmingly small percentage of college athletes actually graduate. A study at one Big 10 university found that while the normal graduation rate was 70 percent, fewer than half of the athletes received degrees. Moreover, only 38 percent of the black athletes had graduated. Another study showed that several western college football powerhouses graduated fewer than 30 percent of their senior football players. Thus, unhappily, the lofty ideal of the scholar-athlete often does not extend beyond the silver-tongued pitch of the college recruiter.

Although the problem may be most evident statistically in college, it doesn't start there. Putting young athletes on pedestals and granting them special favors may in the long run be a disservice to them. Be thankful if your youngster does have athletic ability, but at the same time help him or her to develop into a well-rounded person. As valuable as we believe athletics can be for developing youngsters, we do not believe spiritual enrichment, social and academic development, and quality of family life should suffer. Sports can offer both fun and fulfillment, but there is more to life than sports.

Perhaps the best advice we can give is to encourage your child to participate in sports if he or she wishes to, but at the same time do not allow the tail to wag the dog. Help your child to understand that sport participation is not an end in itself, but a means of achieving various goals. Teach your child to enjoy the process of participation for itself rather than to focus on such end-products as victories and trophies. Neither victory nor defeat should be blown out of proportion, and no parent should permit a child to define his or her self-worth purely on the basis of sport performance. By keeping sports in perspective, you can make it a source of personal and family growth.

Providing and Supporting Alternatives

The development of the child as a well-rounded person is best served by participation in a variety of activities. Thus, part of putting sports in perspective involves encouraging and allowing your youngster to grow in a variety of directions, one of which might well be sports participation. But there are two important instances in which sports are not an option in the child's life: One is when a child decides that he or she does not wish to participate; the other occurs when a child is prevented from participating.

In accordance with the "Bill of Rights for Young Athletes" presented in Chapter 1, we support the basic right of every child to participate in athletics. Sometimes, however, children make the decision not to play. When this happens many parents are confused and disappointed, particularly if they have looked forward to their child's involvement in sports. It is hard under these circumstances to respect a child's decision, but in many cases it is very important to do so.

If your child decides not to participate, the most important first step is to find out why.

Tell your child that you believe it's an important part of growing up to take responsibility for one's own decisions, but that you wish to understand the reasons why he or she doesn't want to play. You need to find out whether the child's decision is based on a lack of interest in the sport or whether it is based on other considerations. For example, some children would actually like to play but decide not to because they don't have confidence in their level of ability or in their acceptance by their teammates. Thus, the most important factor is to decide whether the child would actually like to play. If so, then you as a parent may be able to reassure and encourage your child to give it a try and see how things work out. You should point out to your young athlete that skill levels will increase through participation and that the job of the coach is to help team members become the very best athletes they can.

Sometimes a young athlete decides not to participate because of fear that he or she might let parents down or lose their approval by not performing well enough. If this is the case, you have a golden opportunity to deepen your relationship with your child by exploring his or her feelings and clarifying your own values and expectations. You must face head-on the concern that your child has and the extent to which it is based on reality. The fear may be based on the child's realistic perception of what you expect from him or her. If so, some adjustments in your own thinking may be important. Are you willing to accept your child for what he or she is? Can you love your little bench warmer? Can you be satisfied with your child merely striving to become the best he or she can be, not only in sports but in other activities? If so, and if you can communicate this honestly to your child, this lesson can contribute to lifelong growth.

What to Do If Your Youngster Wants to Quit

At one time or another and for a variety of reasons, most athletes think about quitting. Sometimes a decision to quit comes as a shock to parents, but at other times the warning signs leading up to the decision are very clear.

What are the causes of dropping out of youth sports? In general, the reasons fall into two categories. The first category involves a shift in interests, especially in adolescents. Other involvements, such as a job, a boyfriend or girlfriend, or recreational pursuits, may leave little time for sport involvement. In such cases, a youngster may simply choose to set other priorities.

The second general set of reasons why youngsters drop out relates to negative sports experiences. Research conducted in the

United States and Canada has shown that the following reasons often underlie a decision to drop out:

• Not getting to play

• Undesirable, abusive coaching practices

• An overemphasis on winning that creates stress and reduces fun

• Overorganization, excessive repetition, and regimentation leading to boredom

• Excessive fear of failure, including frustration or failure to achieve personal or team goals

• Mismatching relative to physical size and maturation

If the youngster has decided that other activities are more important, his or her priorities should be respected. However, it is wise to provide a reminder that a commitment has been made to the program and to teammates and that athletes owe it to themselves and to others to honor commitments and to finish out the season. This gives the youngster an opportunity to feel good about himself or herself by fulfilling the obligation through the rest of the season—even if the activity itself is no longer pleasurable.

If the decision to quit is based on one or more of the negative factors listed above, there is a legitimate problem. Again, it is very important that you listen to your child and offer understanding and support. Beyond that, you may discuss some ways to resolve the problems that are affecting the desire to participate. As a last resort you may wish to take some active steps to correct the difficulties. This may involve speaking to the coach or league administrators. In talking with your youngster, you should evaluate how intolerable the situation is to him or her and whether the problems can be worked out. In all but the most severe cases, you can point out that a commitment has been made, and you can encourage your youngster to finish out the season.

If the problems are sufficiently severe, the decision to drop out may be in the best interests of the child. In this case, you would want to communicate to your child that although it is important to live up to commitments, you understand that the principle is outweighed by the nature of the problems. If the child does drop out, there may be other opportunities to play in a sport program that doesn't have the negative factors that prompted the decision to quit.

What to Do If Your Child Is Cut from the Team

Heartbreak can be experienced by both child and parent when youngsters are eliminated from sport participation. Surely not all children can be on the team of their choosing, but we believe that every youngster should have a chance to play. Prior to the age of fourteen, the practice of cutting children from sport programs is indefensible. At the high school level it is appropriate to have select leagues to allow gifted athletes to develop their skills. But even at this age, alternative programs should be available for less-talented youngsters who wish to play the sport.

The tragedy of cutting children from sport programs lies in the fact that those cut are almost always the least skilled or those who have discipline problems. It is precisely these children who are in need of an opportunity to grow through sports. Here again, we must choose between a professional model and one devoted to the development of children. Applying the professional model is certain to lead to a lot of disappointed children. As former basketball star Bill Russell described the world of professional sports, "Those who don't make the team get tossed out on the street. It is a very serious business." In choosing a program for your youngster, you should keep this in mind.

Being cut is an unhappy experience at any age.

What should you do if your child is cut from a team? The first thing is to realize that whether or not your child shows it, he or she is likely to feel disappointed, rejected, and perhaps even humiliated. He or she needs your support at this very difficult time. You can give support by acknowledging the disappointment felt by the child. Do not tell the child not to be disappointed or make unrealistic excuses for why it happened. All people must learn to face disappointments in life. You can make this easier if you show that your love and esteem for him or her has not diminished.

In addition to communicating your understanding acceptance to the child and providing reassurance, you can help your child become involved in other programs or other activities. Help your child to investigate options in other programs in the same sport or in other sports. One child who was at first devastated by being cut from a peewee football team was helped by his parents to get involved in a soccer program and is now having a great time. Your child might also choose a nonathletic activity. If so, that decision should be supported.

Being cut from a team may be particularly painful at the high school level. Moreover, youngsters in this age range, particularly boys, may be unwilling to openly express the hurt they feel. Creating an atmosphere that will help your son explore his feelings may help to ease his sense of rejection.

When Injury Prevents Participation

A young athlete may be temporarily or premanently eliminated from a sport program because of an injury. This may be less painful to the athlete's self-esteem but can in many ways be just as frustrating. For example, a youngster with promising athletic ability can have future hopes dashed by a severe knee or back injury. Here again, parents must try to understand the feelings of frustration, to put up with occasional expressions of this frustration, and to support the youngster through a difficult period. Recognize also that depression, even if not openly expressed, may be reflected in loss of appetite, disturbed sleep patterns, or general apathy. If such symptoms continue or become severe, professional counseling should be pursued.

An injured athlete may require psychological counseling.

If a severe injury occurs to your young athlete, it is very important that he or she be seen by a sports medicine specialist. The possibilities of rehabilitation and complete recovery should not be ruled out without consulting an expert in the field. Sports medicine specialists are experienced in dealing with serious sports-related injuries. Most larger communities have specialized sports medicine clinics devoted to diagnosis, treatment, and rehabilitation.

Helping Your Child Interpret Causes of Sport Outcomes

The judgments we make about the causes of events in our lives are of major importance. In understanding something that happens, we are often asked to decide how much the event was caused by us (factors within ourselves) and how much it was caused by factors outside our control, such as chance or the actions of others. Sport experiences can be an important training ground in forming accurate causal perceptions.

As a parent you can objectively point out what you perceive to be the cause of your child's sport experiences. This can help a youngster form a more realistic way of looking at things. As adults we have our own biases in perception, but we can try to be as objective as possible. For example, if your child blames a loss on a bad call by an umpire or a referee, you might point out that your child did not play up to his or her capabilities. This helps the child evaluate his or her own role in the outcome. On the other hand, a low-self-esteem youngster who blames himself or herself for a defeat may be helped if you point out that the opponent was highly talented and played well that day.

Some parents are quick to protect or comfort their youngsters by blaming others for losses and failures. It may be the coach, teammates, bad luck, or fate. Their children are never faulted for failure to achieve, for it is always due to some external cause. Parents who express such explanations may be doing their children a disservice by communicating that they are never responsible for what happens to them. Such children may begin to view the causes of what

Sports provide an oppurtunity for parent and child to grow closer together.

happens to them as beyond their control. As a result, they may lose sight of the responsibility they have for their own behavior and its consequences.

When parents do help their children to accurately interpret the causes of events, children can develop a balanced perception of reality. This is another way that sports can serve as a valuable arena for learning lessons and acquiring skills that can be applied throughout life. As a parent you can participate in and foster the process.

What to Do After a Tough Loss

Children differ a great deal in their reactions to a loss. Some may be barely affected or may forget the loss almost immediately. Others will be virtually devastated by the loss and may be low-spirited for days.

If your young athlete feels down about a loss, you should give him or her a chance to feel and express the emotion. If, for example, the youngster cries after a loss, this is a realistic expression of depth of feeling and should be accepted as such. At a time like this, a child needs parental support rather than a command to "act like a man."

Respect and acceptance of feeling demands that you not deny or distort what the child is feeling. If your son has struck out three times and made an error that lost the game, he does not want to hear, "You did great." He knows he didn't, and your attempts to comfort him may well come through as a lack of understanding about how he feels. Likewise, it is not very helpful to tell a child that, "It doesn't matter." The fact is that at that moment it does matter a great deal!

Is there anything you can do to make your child feel better without distorting reality? One thing you can do is to point out something positive that was achieved during the contest. A wrestling match may have been lost, but some good takedowns and escapes may have been executed. By emphasizing these accomplishments, you can keep your child from painting a totally negative picture.

Valuable lessons can be learned from both winning and losing.

Another thing that you can do is to look to the future rather than dwell on the loss. Nothing can be done about the loss, so the most productive view is to focus on what has been learned and can be used again.

Above all, don't blame or get angry with the child. He or she feels bad enough already. Support and understanding, sincerely given, will be very helpful at this time.

Perhaps your young athlete plays on a team that loses regularly. If winning is the only goal that is set, your child will be constantly frustrated. If, on the other hand, scaled-down goals are developed, a sense of accomplishment can result as improvement occurs. Knowledgeable coaches often use individual and team goal setting to create a kind of game within the game. For example, the team objective may be to reduce the number of errors, strikeouts, fumbles, or penalties in the next few games. Even if games are lost, children can experience a sense of accomplishment as they attain modified goals.

You can promote similar goal setting on an individual level with your child. In addition to performance goals, you can place emphasis on such important ingredients to success as effort and teamwork. Many a team and many an athlete have been helped to feel as if progress was made toward a larger objective when they succeeded at smaller subgoals.

How to Deal with a Winning Streak

Strangely enough, winning can create its own problems. One is overconfidence and the well-known swelled head. Unless carefully handled, winning teams can become abusive to teams they defeat. And a long winning streak can provide pressures of its own when the emphasis becomes the outcome rather than the process of competition.

When a win occurs, the most natural thing is to enjoy it.

Youngsters should be allowed to feel good about winning—they've earned it. But they should also be reminded to show consideration for their opponents. Emphasize that it never feels good to lose and there is no justification for rubbing it in. Instead, tell youngsters to be gracious winners and to give their opponents a pat on the back or a handshake in a sincere manner.

During a winning streak, most athletes experience not only the pleasure of winning but also the increased pressure not to lose. An additional danger is that if a team wins too regularly and too easily, they may get bored and take their success for granted. A focus on effort and continued improvement can provide an additional and meaningful goal for youngsters. It is important to communicate that you expect continual striving for improvement. Again, winning is to be sought, but it is not the only objective. Finally, don't allow your youngster to rest on past laurels. Point out that past success does not constitute a guarantee of no mistakes or losses in the future.

Parental Behavior at Practices and Games

In Miami, Florida, directors of a youth baseball program found it necessary to move games to midafternoon and to prohibit parents from attending them because of repeated unruly behavior on the part of spectators, including profanity and the physical assault of an umpire.

Near Hilo, Hawaii, a dispute among the parents of rival peewee football teams spilled over into a full-scale riot after the game. A group of parents from one town later invaded the other community with lead pipes and baseball bats, inflicting severe damage and injury.

In Talequah, Oklahoma, a district judge ordered a youth baseball player's mother to stand trial for murder after she fatally shot another player's aunt at a baseball game. The mother, a special-education teacher, shot the other woman after the aunt made derogatory remarks about her son's playing ability.

In parts of New York City, high school basketball games are played in locked gyms with no spectators to protect players and officials from violence.

"I've watched games where little kids were trying to play while parents were screaming from the stands, 'Show some guts.' That made me sick. It's not fun for little kids to play the game under pressure like that."
Billy Martin, major league baseball manager

Much of the job of being a youth sport parent comes from watching your child practice and compete in games and meets. Most children also appreciate their parents' interest and attendance. What youngster isn't bolstered by looking up into the stands and seeing Mom and Dad in rapt attention?

It is most unfortunate when incidents such as those described above occur. Fortunately, the vast majority of parents behave appropriately at youth sport events. But the minority who misbehave can spoil it for all the rest. It takes only a few inconsiderate parents to turn what should be a pleasant atmosphere into one that is stressful for all concerned.

Program directors, game officials, and the participants themselves have a right to demand that spectators observe certain standards of behavior. Two prominent sport scientists, Rainer Martens of the University of Illinois and Vern Seefeldt of Michigan State University, suggest the following minimum guidelines:

- Parents should remain seated in the spectator area during the contest.

- Parents should not yell instructions or criticisms to the children.

- Parents should make no derogatory comments to athletes, parents of the opposing team, officials, or league administrators.

- Parents should not interfere with their children's coach. They must be willing to relinquish the responsibility for their child to the coach for the duration of the contest.

Although they may appear totally engrossed in the game, many children are very sensitive to what is being said from the stands. Laughing or poking fun at an athlete who makes a mistake may inject some humor for the spectators, but it may be heartbreaking for the child. Likewise, "bench jockeying," or attempts to rattle the opposition, is inappropriate at the youth sport level. Indeed, one can question whether such actions are in good taste at any level.

It is easy to get caught up in the action of the game and to suddenly find yourself verbally participating. Parents should never shout criticism or instruction at their children. This applies also to teammates and opponents. If you wish to shout encouragement or praise, make sure that your positive approach extends to the other players as well. But again, codes of sportsmanship dictate that recognition be given to opponents as well. There is no reason why a great play or a great effort made by the opposition should not also be appreciated.

Children are not the only ones who are the targets of barbed comments. Some onlookers seem to forget that youth sport programs could not exist without volunteer coaches and officials who give unselfishly of their time and energy. They deserve your respect

A Little Boy

He stands at the plate with his heart pounding fast; the bases are loaded; the die has been cast.
Mom and dad cannot help him, he stands all alone.
A hit at this moment would send the winning run home.
The ball nears the plate, he swings, but he misses; there's a groan from the crowd with boos and some hisses.
A thoughtless voice shouts, "Strike out, you bum."
Tears fill his eyes; the game's no longer fun.
Remember, he's just a little boy who stands all alone.
So open your heart and give him a break, for it's moments like this a man you can make.
Keep this in mind when you hear someone shout;
Remember, he's still a little boy and not a man yet.
                                        Anonymous

give unselfishly of their time and energy. They deserve your respect and support, and they should be treated with dignity. As tempting as it may be, it is simply not appropriate to second-guess, yell instructions, or disagree with decisions made by the coach.

It is as American as apple pie to boo and criticize judgments made by officials. But such behavior has no place at the youth sport level. Officials are human, and they make mistakes. Like your child, they are amateurs. The officials are honestly trying to do their best. Booing their decisions will not change the outcome or improve the situation in any way. Moreover, parents who "get on" officials provide very poor models for their children, and such behavior can prove highly embarrassing to the young athlete.

Good sportsmanship among spectators is a goal worth working for. We believe that it is the job of parents not only to keep tabs on their own behavior, but also to remind others, if necessary. Coaches and officials have a big enough job without having to police spectators. The rule of thumb for all spectators is that nothing in their actions should interfere with any child's enjoyment of the sport.

Getting Along with Your Child's Coach

Some of the knottiest problems that arise in youth sports involve the relationship between parents and coaches. Any time another significant adult enters your child's world, it may require an adjustment on your part. First of all, as we mentioned in

Parents should be aware of how their children are being coached.

hero. You must also be willing to give up some control and influence in an important area of your youngster's life. Taking a back seat to another adult, even temporarily, isn't always easy. But things can get even more complicated and challenging if you find yourself at odds with coaching decisions that affect your young athlete.

Your responsibility for what happens to your child does not stop when he or she enters a sport program or joins a team. As a parent you have every right to be involved in and to look out for your child's welfare. The tricky part comes in deciding how and to what extent it is appropriate for you to be involved. When does appropriate concern become interference and meddling? At what point must your understandable concern with the happiness and well-being of your child be tempered by respect and understanding for the role of the coach? What should you do if issues like the following crop up?

- Your child isn't getting to play enough during games.

- Your child is not playing the position best suited to his or her talents.

- The coach is mistreating youngsters either verbally or physically.

- The coach is engaging in inappropriate behavior, such as bad language or hazing of officials or opponents.

- The coach is using technically incorrect, questionable, or possibly dangerous coaching methods.

- The coach is demanding too much time or commitment from the youngsters, such that the sport is interfering with other activities.

- The coach is losing perspective of the purpose of youth sports and seems preoccupied with winning, thus putting additional stress on athletes.

Because each situation is somewhat unique, there are no cut-and-dried answers that apply to every case. Nonetheless, there are some general principles that can be helpful in approaching and resolving such problems.

When incidents such as those listed above occur, it would be a mistake not to consider them problems. Perhaps the best starting point is to view them as problems that you and the coach must work on together to resolve. The key to doing so is establishing communication and then keeping the lines of exchange open.

Many parents first become aware of problems when their children complain about the coach. If this happens, the first step is to sit down with your youngster and discuss the problem to get his or her point of view. You should listen and express concern, but do not form a judgment or make condemning statements about the coach. After listening, you may decide that the issue does not warrant your involvement and that it might best be worked out by your youngster and the coach. You can help your child by giving suggestions on how to approach the coach and express concerns. If you can help resolve the issue without your direct involvement, your child may learn some very important interpersonal skills and gain confidence in his or her problem-solving ability.

If the situation seems to warrant it, you should contact the coach and indicate that you would like to have a conference. Such discussions should never occur during practices or games and should not include the child. Having your child there may put the coach on the defensive and create an adversary relationship between you and the coach. What is needed is a mutual problem-solving approach.

Communication is the key to friendly, productive relations with coaches.

When you meet with the coach, you can help create a positive atmosphere for exchange by telling the coach that you appreciate his or her interest in the children and contributions to the program. You might also communicate that you understand how demanding the role of a coach is. In other words, try to create an open and receptive atmosphere for discussion.

Next, indicate that there is an issue that you would like to discuss with the coach and that if there is a problem, you would like to work with the coach in resolving it. Here are some examples of ways in which you can introduce the problem:

Jason told me that he would like to get to play more during games. He feels that since he comes to every practice and tries hard, he'd like to get to play more. (Note that the coach is not being directly accused of not playing Jason enough, which might create defensiveness. Whenever possible, frame the problem in terms of a positive goal to be achieved.)

I have been to several of your basketball practices, and I have seen the drill where you have the children practice taking charging fouls and being run over by an offensive player. I am concerned about the possibility of injury. Is there a safer drill that could be substituted?

I've seen some of the kids get very upset after being yelled at, and I am concerned. I wonder if there isn't some way of making it more fun for the kids. Sometimes we adults don't realize how easy it can be to hurt feelings.

Sara joined the program because she wanted to have fun and because she enjoys playing softball. There seems to be such an emphasis on winning and so much pressure put on the girls to perform that at least for Sara, it's becoming stressful rather than constructive.

After expressing your concern, you might once again acknowledge what a difficult job coaching is, but that you thought the coach would want to hear about your concern because you believe he or she has the best interests of the children at heart. Then tell the coach that you would like to hear his or her view of the situation. Again, the emphasis should be on resolving the problem together.

Communication is a two-way street. You will need to be prepared to listen honestly and openly to the coach's point of view. For example, his or her opinion of your child's ability and deserved playing time may be somewhat different from your own. And the role of coach requires that he or she make a judgment about playing time.

Parents who voice their concerns are often surprised when they are asked to participate in a solution to the problem. For example, one father who disagreed with the coach's way of teaching a particular skill was asked by the coach to assume the position of assistant coach. The coach acknowledged that he had little experience in that particular area and that he would appreciate the father's assistance. In another instance a mother who expressed concern that her son was not playing enough was asked by the coach to practice with the son so that he would improve enough to play more. Thus, we must sometimes be prepared to contribute time and effort as well as opinion.

In some cases you may find that it isn't possible to correct the situation with the coach. If you feel strongly enough about the issue and are convinced that the coach's actions affect the physical or psychological well-being of the children, you may need to take further action. Several options are available.

- First, you may appeal to a higher authority. If a coach is being abusive to children, for example, this should be brought to the attention of league administrators.

- If the issue concerns only your child and not others, the solution may be to request a transfer to another team and coach.

- The last, most drastic, and least desirable alternative may be to remove your child from the program. This should always be a last resort, because it may have some negative consequences of its own. For example, the child may be called a quitter.

Fortunately, most coaches are firmly committed to providing the best possible experiences for youngsters. When approached properly, they will usually be open to parents' concerns and motivated to deal effectively with problems.

Up to now, we have been focusing on undesirable things that might come to your attention. But relating to your child's coach goes beyond this. When things are going well, it is important to offer your support, encouragement, and appreciation to the coach. This adult is playing an important role in your child's life. All too often, the only feedback coaches get from parents is negative. It is important to let them know when they are doing a good job. They deserve it.

Giving Attention to the Nonathlete in the Family

Children who are heavily involved or gifted in athletics have no problem getting lots of attention. In some families, so much attention is paid to the star athlete that brothers and sisters may fade into the background. This is most likely to happen when parents are heavily invested in sports themselves and prize athletic accomplishments. It is important to keep in mind that all children need attention, love, and support from parents. When nonathletes feel pushed into the background, parents may find themselves having to deal with jealousy, feelings of rejection, and lowered self-esteem.

Find something special in each of your children to love and celebrate.

Although involvement in sports is to be encouraged and valued, other areas of achievement should be given equal billing. The nonathletic brother who is trying hard in school or is musically inclined or has a knack for making friends deserves recognition and support just as the young athlete does. Try to impress on your children that each of them has unique gifts and endearing qualities and that you are aware of them. Also emphasize that growing up involves finding out which things children are best at and enjoy most.

Approval of each child as an individual lays the foundation for self-acceptance in all of your children.

Your involvement with your young athlete may vary in degree, but it will almost certainly require a time commitment on your part. This should not detract from personal time with the nonathletic children in your family. We frequently suggest to parents that they keep a daily record of the amount of time spent with each of their children over a two-week period. They are often surprised to find that a huge amount of time is spent on the activities of the young athlete. If you find this to be the case in your family, you may wish to block special time around the activities and interests of your other children. When this is done, no child in the family will feel left out.

Helping Your Marriage Survive Youth Sports

Youth sports can be an important element in family growth and solidarity. Anytime parents share significant experiences with their children, they can help build stronger family ties. Stronger bonds can be forged not only between the parents and children but also between the parents themselves. The sport environment is a place where you and your spouse can witness and enjoy the growth and development of your child. You cannot sit in a classroom and watch academic skills blossom. But you can have a sideline seat to the development of your child's athletic and social skills. Take advantage of the opportunity.

As you are well aware, having children can place certain strains on a marriage. The coming of a child into your relationship means increased demands on time and effort. Children are very needy, and your attention and devotion are the foundation of good parenting. Each phase through which a child develops places different stresses and requirements on you and your spouse. As a result, parents find that they have less time for themselves and for their spouses. Just as youth sports can be a double-edged sword to the athlete, so it can affect husband-wife relationships in a positive or negative fashion. Couples need to be aware of this fact and to be prepared to counteract the potential pitfalls.

**Children not only are a blessing but also offer
special challenges to a marriage.**

Many couples center their lives on thier children and are unaware that their relationship is remaining static or perhaps even crumbling from lack of attention. Many couples unwittingly drift apart during the child-rearing years only to find at the midlife crisis that they have little left in common except their children. Couples now find that they have become married singles. They become absorbed in their day-to-day activities and come to discover that the excitement of their earlier years together has died. On the surface all appears tranquil. The serenity comes from a lack of awareness of what is missing in the relationship. The escalating divorce rate and the number of single-parent families provide grim evidence of this.

Your entry into a youth sport program can free up more time for you and your spouse, or it can place even greater demands on your marriage. As parents discover, there can be an increased time commitment to such things as driving children to and from practices and games, serving on parent committees, or acting as coaches. Some parents find to their dismay that practices are held during the dinner hour and that their kitchen becomes a cafeteria with several shifts. The fun and togetherness of family meals become a thing of the past. For most families this is only a seasonal happening. But for others whose youngsters have year-round involvements, this becomes the normal pattern of living.

Families whose children are in elite individual sports, such as gymnastics, swimming, or figure skating, often bear an extremely heavy responsibility. One mother whose daughter is an up-and-coming figure skater rises each morning at 3:00 A.M. to take her daughter to the rink for practice. This family spends up to $20,000 per year on lessons, ice time, travel to competitions, and equipment. Because of these time and financial commitments, the family has not had a vacation in five years.

To the extent that a sport program does detract from family togetherness, it is important to have family time to make up for time spent apart. When a child is involved in games and practices several nights a week, parents should make it a point to spend Saturday and/or Sunday together as a family.

For some couples, youth sports become a deceptive blessing. Such couples avoid facing problems in their marriage through youth sport involvement. The focus of their lives becomes the child in the athletic arena, and they become so wrapped up in his or her activities that they avoid dealing with marital discord.

Perhaps the most important thing is to decide exactly what your priorities are and what you want out of the sport experience, not only for your child but also for the rest of the family. If your priorities are to grow closer as a family, then you need to think of ways in which you can use sports to improve and not damage this process. For example, are you willing to put up with the chaotic family-dinner schedule that often results? Some parents have answered this question with a firm *no* and have allowed their children to participate in only those programs that do not interfere with the routines of family life.

In most instances, you will have to balance the negative against the positive things that your child and the family might experience in a sport program. Be aware of what is likely to be required and how much time and effort you are willing to devote. Once into a program, you should also keep in mind that you can easily be seduced into more and more involvement. You will have to take your turn in car-pooling and you may be asked to perform other duties.

Special challenges arise for husbands and wives when there is a great difference in interest and involvement in sports. For example, if Mom is totally uninterested in baseball and Dad is a baseball fanatic, there is the chance that Dad will get more and more heavily involved while Mom becomes a sport widow.

What do couples do, then, to compensate for the demands that youth sports can make on their relationship? It is important that parents give time to their own relationship just as they give time to their children. Private moments spent away from the children can serve to maintain and invigorate your relationship. Recreational pursuits for you and your spouse, an occasional weekend away by yourselves, dinners out, and a cultivation of interests you share in common can help maintain the sparkle in your marriage.

Marital bliss doesn't just happen automatically; it comes from actively working at it.

All couples must continue to find ways to improve communication. Get into the habit of talking regularly about your thoughts and, especially, your feelings. As long as the lines of exchange are kept open and problems are openly discussed, your relationship with your loved ones cannot only endure, but can deepen.